BASIC GRAMMAR AND USAGE

FIFTH EDITION

BASIC GRAMMAR AND USAGE

FIFTH EDITION

PENELOPE CHOY
Los Angeles City College

DOROTHY GOLDBART CLARK
Loyola Marymount University

JAMES R. McCORMICK
Skagit Valley College

Harcourt Brace College Publishers

Fort Worth   Philadelphia   San Diego   New York   Orlando   Austin   San Antonio
Toronto   Montreal   London   Sydney   Tokyo

Publisher: Earl McPeek
Executive Editor: Carol Wada
Product Manager: Ilse Wolfe West
Project Editor: Travis Tyre
Production Manager: Linda McMillan
Art Director: Sue Hart

ISBN: 0-15-503634-3
Library of Congress Catalog Card Number: 97-74036
Copyright © 1998, 1994, 1990, 1983, 1978 by Harcourt Brace & Company

Requests for permission to make copies of any part of the work should be mailed to: Permissions Department, Harcourt Brace & Company, 6277 Sea Harbor Drive, Orlando, Florida 32887-6777.

Address for orders:
Harcourt Brace & Company
6277 Sea Harbor Drive
Orlando, FL 32887-6777
1-800-782-4479

Address for editorial correspondence:
Harcourt Brace College Publishers
301 Commerce Street, Suite 3700
Fort Worth, TX 76102
1-800-447-9479

Web site address:
http://www.hbcollege.com

Harcourt Brace & Company will provide complimentary supplements or supplement packages to those adopters qualified under our adoption policy. Please contact your sales representative to learn how you qualify. If as an adopter or potential user you receive supplements you do not need, please return them to your sales representative or send them to: Attn: Returns Department, Troy Warehouse, 465 South Lincoln Drive, Troy, MO 63379.
Printed in the United States of America

7 8 9 0 1 2 3 4 5 6 067 9 8 7 6 5

Preface to the Fifth Edition

In writing the fifth edition of *Basic Grammar and Usage,* we have retained the basic format of earlier editions while making improvements and adding new elements. First, all of the exercises in this edition are new, and as in previous editions, most are in the narrative form which has been so popular with the students and instructors who have used previous editions of our book. Also, several sets of exercises were developed around the themes of popular culture and popular culture interpretation. We believe that these exercises will engage students' interests as well as model critical thinking and interpretative processes.

To encourage students to apply their grammar and usage knowledge more directly to their writing, we have also included a set of new materials to help students edit their work. These include *essays* to be edited (at the end of Units 2, 3, 4, 5, and 6); a *chart* for students to track the kinds of errors they make in their compositions; and *suggestions* for proofreading. The composition editing chart on the inside back cover includes lesson numbers corresponding to each error.

Each lesson contains three end-of-the-chapter exercises in addition to brief exercises within the text. The "A" exercises emphasize the material presented in that particular lesson. The "B" exercises include a review of previous lessons in the same unit. The "C" exercises ask students to construct sentences of their own. A comprehensive unit review exercise appears at the end of each unit. Answers to the "A" exercises appear at the back of the book so students can check their own work. Answers to the "B" and "C" exercises are in the Instructor's Manual.

The Instructor's Manual accompanying *Basic Grammar and Usage* contains a brief diagnostic test for each unit so that the instructor can quickly determine which units each student may need to cover more extensively. A matching achievement test, identical in format to the diagnostic test, can be given at the end of the unit to show exactly how much the student has learned. Longer unit tests are included for instructors who want a more comprehensive exam. All of these tests are printed on easily reproducible eight and one-half by eleven inch pages.

We are grateful to the following colleagues who have provided valuable feedback to help us prepare for this edition: Toni Robinson, Mohave Community College; Edwin Stieve, Nova Southeastern University; and Christian Davis, Bethel College. In addition, we are grateful to the people at Harcourt Brace College Publishers who have helped in the production of this edition: Carol Wada, acquisitions editor; Linda McMillan, production manager; Travis Tyre, project editor; and Sue Hart, art director.

Penelope Choy thanks her husband, Gene Rothman; Dorothy Clark wishes to thank her children, Julia and Benjamin Clark; Kevin O'Neill; and colleagues at Loyola Marymount University (and especially Maria Jackson) for their patience and support during the preparation of the fifth edition.

Our deepest thanks also go to the instructors who have encouraged and supported this book, many of whom have used *Basic Grammar and Usage* since its first appearance in 1978. And to those who first encountered this book as students and are now using it in their own classrooms, we are pleased to serve a second generation of instructors.

Penelope Choy
Dorothy Goldbart Clark

Preface to
the First Edition

Basic Grammar and Usage was originally written for students in a special admissions program at the University of California, Los Angeles. As part of their participation in the program, the students were enrolled in a composition and grammar course designed to prepare them for the university's freshman English courses. When the program began in 1971, none of the grammar textbooks then on the market seemed suitable for the students, whose previous exposure to grammar had been cursory or, in some cases, nonexistent. As the director of the program's English classes, I decided to write a book of my own that would cover the most important areas of grammar and usage in a way that would be easily understood by my students.

The original version of *Basic Grammar and Usage* received an enthusiastic response from the students and was used successfully throughout the three-year duration of the program. After the program ended in 1974, many of the instructors asked permission to reproduce the book for use in their new teaching positions. By the time copies of *Basic Grammar and Usage* reached Harcourt Brace Jovanovich in 1975, the text had already been used by more than 1,500 students in nearly a dozen schools.

Basic Grammar and Usage presents material in small segments so that students can master a particular topic one step at a time. The lessons within each unit are cumulative. For example, students doing the pronoun exercises for Lesson 19 will find that those exercises include a review of the constructions treated in Lessons 16 to 18. This approach reinforces the students' grasp of the material and helps them develop the skills they need for the writing of compositions. To make them more interesting to students, the exercises in four of the six units are presented as short narratives rather than as lists of unrelated sentences. Each lesson concludes with two exercises, which may be either used in class or assigned as homework. In addition, each unit ends with a composition that the students must proofread for errors and then correct to demonstrate mastery of the material.

Students who have never before studied grammar systematically will find that working through the text from beginning to end provides an insight into the basic patterns of English grammar. As one student commented on an end-of-course evaluation, "The most important thing I learned from *Basic Grammar and Usage* is that if you learn what an independent clause is, half of your grammar problems are over." On the other hand, students who do not need a total review of grammar can concentrate on the specific areas in which they have weaknesses. To help the instructor evaluate both types of student, the Instructor's Manual accompanying the text includes a diagnostic test and a post-test divided into sections corresponding to the units in the book. There are also separate achievement tests for each unit, as well as answer keys to the exercises presented in the text.

Although *Basic Grammar and Usage* is designed for students whose native language is English, it has been used successfully by students learning English as a second language. In addition to being a classroom text, *Basic Grammar and Usage* can be used in writing labs and for individual tutoring.

Many people have shared in the preparation of *Basic Grammar and Usage*. I wish in particular to thank the instructors and administrators of UCLA's Academic Advancement Program, where this book originated. In revising the text for publication, I have been greatly helped by the suggestions of Regina Sackmary of Queensborough Community College of the City University of New York and by Elizabeth Gavin, formerly of California State University, Long Beach, who reviewed the manuscript for me. Sue Houchins of the Black Studies Center of the Claremont Colleges contributed many ideas and reference materials for the exercises. An author could not ask for more supportive people to work with than the staff of Harcourt Brace Jovanovich. I owe a special debt of gratitude to Raoul Savoie, who first brought the UCLA version of the text to the attention of his company. I also wish to thank Lauren Procton, who was responsible for the editing, and Eben W. Ludlow, who has provided guidance and encouragement throughout all the stages of this book's development.

Penelope Choy

To the Student: Using This Book to Edit Your Compositions

Basic Grammar and Usage is designed to help you master the most important rules of grammar, usage, and grammatical structures. However, learning grammar and usage is only a means to an end, not an end in itself. Learning grammar and usage should ultimately enable you to write better compositions—compositions with clearly written and easily understood sentences that are free of distracting errors that draw your reader's attention away from the important points you are trying to make.

When you write a composition, the first draft of your paper may not be free of grammar and usage errors. But you can learn to edit your papers; that is, to remove mistakes before you complete the final draft. The first step in this process is for you to know the kinds of mistakes you most often make. Your instructor may give you a pretest to point out areas of grammar and usage that you need to study. You should also keep track of the mistakes you make in your compositions. Then, as you study the lessons, *Basic Grammar and Usage* will explain how to avoid these errors. You can then look for these particular mistakes on the rough drafts of your essays.

The chart displayed on the inside back cover will help you keep track of the kinds of mistakes you make. Your instructor can also supply you with a full-page chart from the *Basic Grammar and Usage* Instructor's Manual. Notice that there are columns in which you may enter the number and kind of mistakes you make on your papers. There is also a list of corresponding lessons in *Basic Grammar and Usage* in which each mistake is discussed.

Editing your papers will be easier if you prepare your manuscript for proof-reading in advance. Whether you are using a typewriter or a word processor, you should triple-space between lines to provide plenty of room to make corrections. If you are writing by hand, write on every other line, and do not write on the back of the page. If you use a word processing software program, it will help to use a large font for your rough draft, to make it easier to read. With a word processor, it is easy to look at one section of a paper at a time. If you are writing by hand, consider writing each paragraph on separate sheets of paper. This way, correcting one paragraph of your essay at a time will not only seem less overwhelming, but it will be easier to completely rewrite a paragraph should you decide it is needed. You will also not have to recopy other parts of the essay.

The authors of *Basic Grammar and Usage* collected the following suggestions (from other English instructors and their best students) to demonstrate how best to edit a paper for grammar and usage errors:

1. Do not try to edit your paper immediately after you finish writing it. Let some time pass so that you do not overlook mistakes because of your familiarity with the paper.
2. Look for one type of error at a time. Try not to proofread for everything at once. For example, if you know that you often write comma splices, check first for that mistake before looking for others.
3. Begin by looking for the mistakes you and/or your instructor consider to be the most serious.
4. Consider reading the paper aloud or recording it into a tape player and listening to it. Read slowly and carefully. If you have any trouble reading the sentences or words, it is a sign that they may be awkwardly written or that they may contain major grammatical errors needing to be corrected.
5. Try reading the paper backwards, from the last sentence to the first. This will help overcome a common problem of overlooking mistakes because you will tend to concentrate on the flow of ideas rather than on the mechanics of the grammar and usage. When you read from the back to the front, the sentences will no longer have a familiar continuity. This will make it easier for you to look at each sentence individually and spot mistakes each sentence may contain.

6. On your last reading, move a ruler down the page as you read from beginning to end. This will help you read more slowly and concentrate better on each sentence.

7. Plan on reading your paper several times: one time for each major kind of error and one time for each major revision of your draft.

8. Plan on spending the time necessary for editing your paper properly. This will include time for taking a break between the time you finish the paper and the time you begin editing it, time for proofreading more than once, and time for a final reading of your last draft.

Contents

BASIC
GRAMMAR
AND
USAGE

FIFTH EDITION

IDENTIFYING SUBJECTS AND VERBS

Sentences with One Subject and One Verb

The most important grammatical skill you can learn is how to identify subjects and verbs. Just as solving arithmetic problems requires you to know the multiplication tables perfectly, solving grammatical problems requires you to identify subjects and verbs with perfect accuracy. This is not as difficult as it sounds. With practice, recognizing subjects and verbs will become as automatic as knowing that $2 + 2 = 4$.

Although in conversation people often speak in short word groups that may not be complete sentences, in written English people usually use complete sentences.

A complete sentence contains at least one subject and one verb.

A sentence can be thought of as a statement describing an *actor* performing a particular *action*. For example, in the sentence "The dog ran," the *actor* or person performing the action is the dog. What *action* did the dog perform? He *ran*. This *actor-action* pattern can be found in most sentences. Can you identify the actor and the action in each of the following sentences?

Harcourt Brace & Company

The teacher laughed.

The crowd applauded.

The *actor* in a sentence is called the **subject.** The *action* word in a sentence is called the **verb.** Together, the subject and verb form the core of the sentence. Notice that even if extra words are added to the two sentences above, the subject-verb core in each sentence remains the same.

The teacher laughed at the student's joke.

After the performance, the crowd applauded enthusiastically.

You can see that in order to identify subjects and verbs, you must be able to separate these core words from the rest of the words in the sentence.

Here are some suggestions to help you identify verbs.

1. The *action* words in sentences are verbs. For example:

The team *played* well.
This store *sells* rare books.
The doctor *recommended* vitamins.

Underline the verb in each of the following sentences.

The bank lends money to small businesses.
Gina speaks Italian.
The flood destroyed many homes.

2. *All forms of the verb* "to be" *are verbs:* am, is, are, was, were, and *been.* For example:

Susan *is* unhappy.
The actor *was* nervous.

Verbs also include words that can be used as substitutes for forms of *be,* such as *seem, feel, become,* and *appear.* These verbs are called **linking or auxiliary verbs.**

Susan *seems* unhappy.
The actor *appeared* nervous.

Harcourt Brace & Company

Underline the verb in each of the following sentences.

The children became excited during the birthday party.
The professor seemed fatigued today.
The actors felt happy about their performance.

3. Verbs are the only words that change their spelling to show tense. **Tense** is the time—present, past, or future—at which the verb's action occurs. For example, the sentence "We *walk* each morning" has a present-tense verb. The sentence "We *walked* each morning" has a past-tense verb. Underline the verb in each of the following sentences.

Grandfather moves today.
My brother moved to Chicago last month.
Sandra dances very well.
Maria danced with a ballet company.
I wash my hair every morning.
The nurse washed her hands.

Identifying verbs will be easier for you if you remember that the following kinds of words are *not* verbs.

4. An **infinitive**—the combination of the word *to* plus a verb, such as *to walk* or *to study*—is not considered part of the verb in a sentence. Read the following sentences.

He plans to swim later.
She wants to enter graduate school.

The main verbs in these two sentences are *plans* and *wants*. The infinitives *to swim* and *to enter* are not included. Underline the main verb in each of the following sentences.

Benjy decided to play his new video games.
The conductor promised to check our luggage.

5. **Adverbs**—words that describe a verb—are *not* part of the verb. Many commonly used adverbs end in *-ly*. The adverbs in the following sentences are italicized. Underline the verb in each sentence.

Harcourt Brace & Company

The guitarist played *badly.*
Phillipe rushed *quickly* to our rescue.
The mother *patiently* helped her children.

The words *not, never,* and *very* are also adverbs. Like other adverbs, these words are *not* part of the verb. Underline the verb in each of the following sentences. Do *not* include adverbs.

The dancers are not here yet.
He never studies late.
The director spoke very carefully.
He is not a good mechanic.
José never remembers to close the door.

Now that you can identify verbs, here are some suggestions to help you to identify subjects.

1. The subject of a sentence is most often a noun. A **noun** is the name of a person, place, or thing, such as *Julia, Houston,* or *pens.* A noun may also be the name of an abstract idea, such as *sadness* or *failure.* Underline the subject in each of the following sentences *once* and the verb *twice.* Remember that the verb is the *action,* and the subject is the *actor.*

Kevin reads many books each month.
The store closes at midnight.
Atlanta hosted the 1996 Olympics.
Love conquers all.

2. The subject of a sentence may also be a **subject pronoun.** A **pronoun** is a word used in place of a noun, such as *she* (= *Julia*), *it* (= *Houston*), or *they* (= *pens*). The following words are subject pronouns:

I, you, he, she, it, we, they

Underline the subject in each of the following sentences *once* and the verb *twice.*

He was elected president of the United States.
Each spring they travel to Yosemite.
I always drink strong coffee.

Harcourt Brace & Company

We rarely have dinner out on weekdays.
You washed the dishes last night.

3. The subject of a sentence may also be a **gerund.** A **gerund** is an -ing form of a verb used as a noun. For example, in the sentence "Swimming is an excellent form of exercise," the subject of the sentence is the gerund *swimming.* Underline the gerund subjects in the following sentences *once* and the verbs *twice.*

Listening is difficult for young children.
Dieting makes me very hungry.

4. In **commands** (also known as **imperatives**), such as "Wash the dishes!," the subject is understood to be the subject pronoun *you* even though the word *you* is almost never included in the command. *You* is understood to be the subject of the following sentences.

Do your homework early.
Consider the alternative.

Underline the subject in each of the following sentences *once* and the verb *twice.* If the sentence is a command, write the subject *you* in parentheses at the beginning of the sentence.

Remember to wipe your feet before entering.
The judge reviewed the verdict.
They bowl every Wednesday.
Discuss these issues with your colleagues.

Identifying subjects will be easier for you if you remember that the following kinds of words are *not* subjects.

5. **Adjectives**—words that describe a noun—are *not* part of the subject. For example, in the sentence "The tall boy runs well," the subject is "boy," *not* "tall boy." In the sentence "A new car is a great joy," the subject is "car," *not* "new car." Underline the subject in each of the following sentences *once* and the verb *twice.*

A talented singer performed that song.
Chocolate cake is his favorite food.

Small pets delight our family.
An angry, bitter debate ended the program.

6. Words that show **possession,** or ownership, are *not* part of the subject. Words that show possession include nouns ending in an apostrophe (') combined with *s,* such as *Dina's* or *cat's.* They also include **possessive pronouns,** words that replace nouns showing ownership, such as *his* (= *Dina's*) or *its* (= *cat's*). Possessive pronouns include the following words:

my, your, his, hers, its, our, their

Since words that show possession are *not* part of the subject, in the sentence "My dog has fleas," the subject is "dog," *not* "my dog." In the sentence "Sarah's mother is a doctor," the subject is "mother," *not* "Sarah's mother." Underline the subject in each of the following sentences *once* and the verb *twice.*

His daughter became a doctor.
My brother works in another city.
This beach's beauty is startling.
Harry's car needs a new battery.

Here is a final suggestion to help you identify subjects and verbs accurately.

Try to identify the verb in a sentence before you try to identify the subject.

A sentence may have many nouns, any of which could be the subject, but it will usually have only one or two verbs.

For example:

The director of the play shouted angry words to all the actors and staff.

There are five nouns in the above sentence (*director, play, words, actors, staff*), any of which might be the subject. However, there is only one verb– *shouted.* Once you have identified the verb as *shouted,* all you have to ask yourself is "Who or what shouted?" The answer is *director,* which is the subject of the sentence.

Identify the subject and verb in the following sentence, remembering to look for the verb first.

In the winter, we travel to the mountains for our vacation.

Remember these basic points:

1. The action being performed in a sentence is the **verb.**
2. The person or thing performing the action is the **subject.**
3. A sentence consists of an *actor* performing an *action,* or, in other words, a **subject** plus a **verb.**

Since every sentence you write will have a subject and a verb, you must be able to identify subjects and verbs in order to write correctly. Therefore, as you do the exercises in this unit, apply the rules you have learned in each lesson, and *think* about what you are doing. Do not make random guesses. Grammar is based on logic, not on luck.

Underline the subject in each of the following sentences *once* and the verb *twice*. Add the subject *you* in parentheses if the sentence is a command.

That man won the contest yesterday.
Success makes us happy.
The ancient horse slowly pulled the cart.
Wisdom is endless.
Consider the virtues of discipline.
My little sister's dance recital was lots of fun.
A quiet garden is my favorite place to read.
Your family's last vacation sounds very exciting.

Underline the subject of each sentence *once* and each verb *twice*. Each sentence has only one subject and one verb. *Remember to look for the verb first* before you try to find the subject.

1. Every country has its own customs.

2. These customs help to shape the behavior of its people.

3. Eating meals at particular times of the day is an example of a custom.

4. Americans traditionally eat three meals a day.

5. Each meal features different kinds of food.

6. American breakfasts generally include cereal, eggs, or bread.

7. Few people expect to eat soup early in the morning.

8. However, customs vary from country to country.

9. Hot soup for breakfast is not unusual in some Asian countries.

10. Customs also change over time.

11. Today's Americans often lack the time for regular meals.

12. Some busy people nibble on snacks all day long.

13. Today, snacks often substitute for the regular mealtimes of the past.

14. Customs are an important part of a society's culture.

15. Culture also includes things like art, music, and literature.

16. Many exercises in this book describe aspects of current American culture, from rock music to self-help books.

17. Looking at our current culture helps us to understand patterns of change in our society.

Underline the subject of each sentence *once* and the verb *twice*. Each sentence has one subject and one verb. *Remember to look for the verb first* before you try to locate the subject.

1. Today, many scholars study popular culture.

2. Popular culture reflects a society's values and beliefs.

3. In fact, many things in our culture send "signs" or messages to us.

4. Scholars interpret these "signs."

5. For example, television shows reveal much about us.

6. The more recent *Roseanne* presents a very different family than the earlier *Father Knows Best*.

7. Dad in *Father Knows Best* was the beloved head of the family.

8. Mom just stayed home.

9. The children respected their mom and dad.

10. Everyone acted politely to one another.

11. The family in *Roseanne* is very different.

12. For example, Mom works as a waitress.

13. Sometimes, Dad knows very little about handling the children.

14. Politeness rarely appears in this family.

15. The children often talk rudely to their parents.

16. Almost no difference in status exists between the parents and the children.

17. *Roseanne* is more than "realistic" television.

18. To many social critics, *Roseanne* suggests trends in the American family.

19. *The Simpsons* also teaches us something about American families.

20. Bart Simpson provides a very different role model from sons in earlier family shows.

21. Homer Simpson is nothing like the father in *Father Knows Best.*

22. Homer Simpson's foolishness suggests changes in the role of the father and the traditional family.

23. Television shows are one important area of popular culture studies.

Harcourt Brace & Company

Each group of words below can be made into a complete sentence by the addition of *one* word. The missing word may be a subject (a noun or a subject pronoun), or it may be a verb. Make each group of words a sentence by adding either a *one-word subject* or a *one-word verb*.

1. _____ with caution.

2. Julia _____ 1500 sit-ups every night!

3. My _____ need lots of attention.

4. The man _____ the dishes.

5. Bianca's _____ is a lawyer.

6. Sergio _____ every day.

7. Buffalo, New York _____ very cold.

8. The nurse _____ the child's temperature.

9. Kevin _____ the bagpipes.

10. _____ plays the piano.

11. The teacher _____ the problem for us.

12. Sarah _____ Pedro the briefcase.

13. _____ to brush your teeth at night.

Multiple Subjects and Verbs

Some sentences have more than one subject. Others have more than one verb. Many sentences have more than one subject *and* more than one verb. The subjects in the following sentences have been labeled with an "S" and the verbs with a "V."

   S   V   V
He swam and fished this summer.

      S   S   V
The dog and kitten became good friends.

   S   V   S   V
She danced well, and the director applauded.

      S   V   S   V
When we study hard, we usually do well.

You can identify the pattern of a sentence by indicating how many subjects and verbs it has. Although in theory a sentence can have any number of subjects and verbs, these are the most common patterns:

S-V	one subject and one verb
S-V-V	one subject and two verbs
S-S-V	two subjects and one verb
S-V/S-V	two subjects and two verbs

Underline the subjects of the following sentences *once* and the verbs *twice*.

The parrot squawked loudly.

His job started early and ended quite late.

Gardening and decorating were Beatrice's joys.

The team won the game, yet the captain was not happy.

Any group of words that contains *at least one subject and one verb* is called a **clause.** A single sentence may have one clause or more than one clause.

S-V	one clause	The boy ate his pizza slice.
S-V-V	one clause	Sonja danced and sang.
S-S-V	one clause	The judge and jury joked.
S-V/S-V	two clauses	The dog barked, / and we laughed.
S-V-V/S-V	two clauses	He hiked and fished / when the sun rose.

Later in the book we will study the different types of clauses to understand how they determine punctuation. But for now the important thing is to learn to find all the subjects and verbs in each sentence.

Something to keep in mind when looking for multiple subjects and verbs is that the *length* of the sentence won't tell you whether the sentence has one clause or several clauses. Look at these two sentences:

She sang, but I danced. (How many clauses?)

The anxious, nervous young bride tripped on the stair. (How many clauses?)

The first sentence is short, only five words, but it has two S-V patterns and, therefore, two clauses (*she sang,* but *I danced*). The second sentence is more than

Harcourt Brace & Company

twice as long, but it has only one clause (*bride . . . tripped*). So don't be fooled by the length of the sentence: some short sentences have multiple subjects and verbs, and some long sentences have only a single clause (S-V).

The sentences below are skeleton sentences. That is, they are stripped down to only subjects and verbs and connecting words. Go through them underlining the subjects *once* and the verbs *twice*.

Sarah laughed and joked.

Julia and Benjy argued and fought.

The poet, the artist, and the teacher spoke.

After the game ended, we had lunch.

Laughter invigorates, and love binds.

Because it snowed, we stayed home.

When the movie ended, we left.

The philosopher and his ideas were exciting.

As we watched and waited, the river flooded.

If you go, I stay.

Janice wrote and slept.

As we listened, the storyteller entranced us.

He cried while she packed.

Watch your spelling! (Did you remember to put *You* in front?)

The practice sentences below have multiple subjects and verbs, but they also include the other types of words you studied in Chapter 1. Before you try them, review that chapter quickly to remind yourself about **adverbs** and **infinitives,** which are never part of the verb, and about **adjectives** and **possessives,** which are not part of the subject. Underline verbs *twice* and subjects *once:*

Harcourt Brace & Company

My uncles and aunts contribute to our family.

The long road seemed to run on for miles and miles.

Duwane, Jose, and Clarence always loved to play soccer.

The gymnastic tournament finally ended, and the players went home.

After the spring semester ended, we partied a lot.

The terribly boring professor lectured monotonously to his class of students.

The boy's mother and father decided to send him to a space camp.

The jury's verdict gladdened and relieved us.

The story's end surprised us, but we still liked it.

Our new fancy, expensive car has a CD player and a sunroof.

Keep off the grass, and don't pick the flowers!

Underline the subjects of the following sentences *once* and the verbs *twice*. To help you, the pattern of each sentence is indicated in parentheses.

1. Television shows entertain us, but sometimes they are a little deceiving. (S-V/S-V)

2. *Melrose Place* is a show with a slight deception. (S-V)

3. Although the show's characters work all over the city, they all live on Melrose Place. (S-V/S-V)

4. A funny thing and surprising fact about the street also reveal something about television shows. (S-S-V)

5. In reality, Melrose Place has no houses or apartment buildings, and no people actually live there! (S-V/S-V)

6. While Wilshire Blvd. and Sunset Blvd. have many different kinds of buildings, Melrose Place is only a commercial street. (S-S-V/S-V)

7. Antique stores comprise the majority of shops on this street. (S-V)

8. You also find two hair salons and one trendy restaurant on Melrose Place, but no apartments or expensive homes exist. (S-V/S-S-V).

9. One other special store is here, too. (S-V)

10. Although this store is a kind of beauty salon, it provides no hair care. (S-V/S-V)

11. Massages and facials are this salon's specialties. (S-S-V)

12. The owners also dye women's eyelashes. (S-V)

13. Women from all over the Los Angeles area come to this salon to relax on Melrose Place and to become more beautiful. (S-V)

14. Because Melrose Place is the name of a television show, few people realize how tiny it is. (S-V/S-V)

15. Although Wilshire Blvd. and Sunset Blvd. run for miles and miles, Melrose Place is only one short block long! (S-S-V/S-V)

Harcourt Brace & Company

Underline the subjects of the following sentences *once* and the verbs *twice*. Some sentences have more than one subject, more than one verb, or both.

1. We learn a lot about each other from the way we dress.

2. When we choose our clothes, we make a statement about ourselves.

3. For example, some people dress very trendily, and others choose to look traditional.

4. Our clothing, hairstyle, and even our makeup communicate messages to others.

5. If she has multiple piercings, she is identifying with a somewhat rebellious, younger style.

6. In contrast, a person in Dockers and button down shirts suggests a more mainstream style and reflects a more conservative orientation.

7. We often judge people by their appearance, and we sometimes choose to look a certain way in order to communicate a message.

8. Because we choose clothes to project an image, social observers think of our clothing as a kind of language.

9. Gangster-style clothing offers a good example and teaches us a lot about the language of style.

10. Although gangster-style clothing is part of the gang lifestyle of the inner city, many other young people wear this style.

11. You probably know this style well and identify it by its baggy look.

12. Baggy pants and baggy shirts mark the gangster look, and the pants need to "sag"—to be worn very low.

13. This loose clothing style came from prison wear because prisons issued clothing of all sizes to released inmates.

14. Therefore, wearing baggy clothes became a badge of dubious honor for recently released convicts, and others picked up the style as a sign of defiance.

15. So, when non-gangster youths wear and parade this style, they signal an identification with the defiance and toughness of the gangs.

16. Although this example is very dramatic, all styles signal some kind of message to others.

17. Each generation seems to develop a unique style to identify itself, and today's generation finds a variety of styles to make such identity statements.

18. In the sixties, youths wore their hair long as a sign of rebellion while in the nineties, some teenagers color their hair in bright hues, shave their heads, or sometimes carve initials in their hair.

19. Sometimes, we change our styles many times a day and make different statements about ourselves at different times.

20. For example, in the morning I wear flannel clothing to school and listen to grunge music while at night I put on a suit and go to the opera.

21. My daytime friends are very different from my night pals, but I am still me!

22. However, I communicate different attitudes and value systems every time I change my style of clothing.

23. The next time you choose clothes, ask yourself what messages these clothes send.

Harcourt Brace & Company

The following sentences need more than one subject, more than one verb, or both. Put *one* noun, *one* pronoun, or *one* verb in each blank to complete each sentence.

1. _____, _____, and _____ wrote the

   book together.

2. Since _____ bought the groceries, the club _____

   to do the work.

3. The new _____ and baby puppy _____ together

   famously.

4. Several _____ studied for the test, but they _____

   anyway.

5. _____ ran the race and _____ the prize.

6. The unhappy _____ _____ the dog.

7. After _____ saw the movie, he _____ to the

   bus stop.

8. The _____ considered the facts and _____ on the

   issues.

9. My sister _____ dinner, my brother _____ the living room, and I _____ the clothes.

10. Every year, many watch the Academy Awards and then _____

_____ to the movies.

11. The large _____ ran over to see its friend and then it

_____ the fence.

12. As they _____ at the sky, _____ were certain

something flashed overhead.

13. Yesterday the _____ attended the class and _____

the information.

14. _____ remembered the assignment and _____ the

homework late at night.

15. The man _____ the poison and quickly _____.

Distinguishing Between Objects of Prepositions and Subjects

One of the most common causes of errors in identifying the subject of a sentence is confusing it with a noun used as the object of a preposition. This kind of error can also lead to mistakes in subject-verb agreement. (Subject-verb agreement is covered in Unit Two of this book.) To avoid making this type of mistake, you first must learn to recognize prepositions and prepositional phrases.

Prepositions are the short words in our language that show the *position* or relationship between one word and another. For example, if you were trying to describe where a particular store was located, you might say:

The store is *on* the right.

The store is *near* the highway.

The store is *by* the bank.

The store is *under* the elm tree.

The store is *behind* the garage.

Harcourt Brace & Company

The italicized words are all prepositions. They show the position of the store in relation to the right, the freeway the bank the elm tree, and the garage.

Here is a list of the most common prepositions. You do not have to memorize these words, but you must be able to recognize them as prepositions when you see them.

about	between	of
above	beyond	on
across	by	onto
after	concerning	out
against	down	over
along	during	through
amid	except	to
among	for	toward
around	from	under
at	in	up
before	inside	upon
behind	into	with
below	like	within
beneath	near	without
beside		

As you can see from the sentences describing the location of the store, prepositions are not used by themselves; they are always placed in front of a noun or pronoun. The noun or pronoun following the preposition is called the **object of the preposition.** The group of words containing the preposition and its object is called a **prepositional phrase.** Any words, such as adjectives or the words *a, an,* or *the,* which come between the preposition and its object are also part of the prepositional phrase. Read the following sentences, in which the prepositional phrases are italicized. Notice that each prepositional phrase begins with a preposition and ends with a noun or pronoun.

I leaned *against the car.*

He walked *toward the nearest exit.*

The glass *of orange juice* costs fifty cents.

She stood *beside me.*

Some prepositional phrases may have more than one object.

You may sit *near Jane or Susan.*

You may have some *of the bread or waffles.*

It is also possible to have two or more prepositional phrases in a row.

We looked *for the clues in the forest.*

The director *of that movie at the local theater* is sitting by us.

Circle the prepositional phrases in the following sentences. Some sentences may have more than one prepositional phrase.

The policeman looked carefully around the room.

The keys to the car are in the glove compartment.

I gave your recipe to my next-door neighbor.

Ruth came to the party with me.

Construct sentences of your own containing prepositional phrases. Use the prepositions listed below. Make certain that each of your sentences contains at least one subject and one verb.

with: _____

_____

through: _____

_____

by: _____

_____

of: _____

_____

at: _____

_____

The words *before* and *after* may be used either as prepositions or as conjunctions (see below). If the word is being used as a preposition, it will be followed by a noun or pronoun object. If the word is being used as a conjunction, it will be followed by both a subject and a verb.

As a Preposition	*As a Conjunction*
I go to bed *before midnight.*	*Before* you leave the house, be sure to lock the door.
Bob entered the room *after me.*	*After* the bell rang, the students left the room.

What do prepositional phrases have to do with identifying subjects and verbs? The answer is simple.

Any word that is part of a prepositional phrase cannot be the subject or the verb of a sentence.

This rule works for two reasons:

1. Any noun or pronoun in a prepositional phrase must be the object of the preposition, and the object of a preposition cannot also be a subject.
2. Prepositional phrases never contain verbs.

To see how this rule can help you to identify subjects and verbs, read the following seventeen-word sentence:

At the height of the rush hour, my car stalled in the middle of a busy intersection.

If you want to find the subject and verb of this sentence, you know that they will not be part of any of the sentence's prepositional phrases. So, cross out all the prepositional phrases in the sentence.

~~At the height of the rush hour,~~ my car stalled ~~in the middle of a busy intersection.~~

You now have only three words left out of the original seventeen, and you know that the subject and verb must be within these three words. What are the subject and verb?

Read the following sentence, and cross out all of its prepositional phrases.

In the evening she works on her assignments for the next day.

If you crossed out all the prepositional phrases, you should be left with only two words—the subject *she* and the verb *works*.

Identify the subject and verb in the following sentence. Cross out the prepositional phrases first.

On the way to their hotel, a group of tourists stopped at a souvenir shop.

If you have identified all of the prepositional phrases, you should be left with only three words—*a group* and *stopped*. Which word is the subject, and which is the verb?

Now you can see another reason why it is important to be able to identify prepositional phrases. It might seem logical for the subject of the sentence to be *tourists*. However, since *of tourists* is a prepositional phrase, *tourists* cannot be the subject. Instead, the subject is *group*.

What is the subject of the following sentence?

Many members of Congress are lawyers.

If you crossed out the prepositional phrase *of Congress,* you would know that the subject is *members,* not *Congress.*

Underline the subjects of the following sentences *once* and the verbs *twice.* Remember to cross out the prepositional phrases first.

During the oil shortage, the price of gas increased.
The car with the dented fender belongs to Carolyn.
A house in Beverly Hills with three bedrooms and two baths sells for over eight hundred thousand dollars.
The stores in the mall open at ten in the morning.
The driver of the red Corvette skidded into the center lane.
One of the employees received a fifty-dollar raise.
Your clothes from the dry cleaner are in the closet.

Harcourt Brace & Company

Underline the subjects of the following sentences *once* and the verbs *twice*. Some sentences may have more than one subject, more than one verb, or both. Remember to cross out the prepositional phrases first.

1. Some people consider rock music a form of rebellion for young people.

2. In the 1950s, many parents of teenagers objected to singers of a new rock beat.

3. Elvis Presley received the most criticism of these new singers.

4. The parents of the teenagers disliked his sexy movements and hated his singing.

5. In the 1970s, many pop rock and heavy metal groups rebelled against society with outrageous acts.

6. Elton John dressed in elevator shoes and wild, multi-hued glasses.

7. The heavy metal group KISS never appeared in public without heavy black and white makeup on their faces.

8. Nobody ever saw their real faces.

9. Of all the heavy metal singers, Ozzy Osborne is probably the most outrageous.

10. He performs odd and shocking acts in his show.

11. During his concerts, Ozzy Osborne bites the heads off of mice and kills other small creatures.

12. In the late 1990s, Marilyn Manson sings songs about evil and produces a newsletter with an interesting philosophy of skepticism.

13. For its generation, this group exhibits the same nonconformity as Elvis Presley, Elton John, KISS, and Ozzy Osborne.

14. For groups of this kind, it is very important and very necessary to be outrageous.

15. Although this outrageous behavior is usually an act, it is very convincing to many teenagers.

16. Parents of the 1950s hated Elvis.

17. Today, Elvis Presley seems pedestrian in comparison to Marilyn Manson and Ozzy Osborne.

Underline the subjects of the following sentences *once* and the verbs *twice*. Some sentences may have more than one subject, more than one verb, or both. Remember to cross out the prepositional phrases first.

1. One of the most interesting movements in recent times is people's need for a community center of some sort.

2. Many Americans live in large, urban centers, and old-fashioned neighborhoods are hard to find.

3. A lot of people have no contact with people near them.

4. Consequently, dwellers in urban areas often feel very lonely and seek some sort of human connection.

5. The mall in all its glory is one way for urbanites to solve this problem.

6. Some of the most amazing events occur in malls.

7. One of these events at a large urban mall was a baby derby.

8. Babies of all ages and in all sizes crawled toward toys in order to win a contest.

9. People from all over the area brought their babies and watched them.

10. Although this event was funny, in a special way it served some important purposes.

11. In a large metropolitan area, lonely people with children gathered together to laugh at babies with numbers taped to their diapers and to share joy with other parents.

12. Events of all sorts in malls bring people together as communities of the moment.

13. Sometimes communities of the moment occur around entertainment in the mall.

Harcourt Brace & Company

14. From jazz bands to children's performers and storytellers, entertainers at malls draw people to them and create a sense of community connection.

15. Malls now even substitute for old-fashioned neighborhood or family gatherings during the holiday seasons.

16. All of us expect Santa Claus at malls during Christmas, but now even minor holidays get lots of attention, too.

17. For example, at many malls urbanites find actual pumpkin patches at Halloween, and stores supply candy for trick-or-treaters.

18. The malls of today are the community centers of yesterday.

Part One. A prepositional phrase adds more meaning to a sentence, but it also adds a noun or pronoun that may be mistaken for the subject. In each of the following sentences, underline the subject of the sentence *once* and the verb *twice*. Then *add* a prepositional phrase between the subject and the verb. The first sentence has been done as an example.

       about our class
1. A <u>story</u> ^ <u><u>won</u></u> the prize.

2. The gift was expensive.

3. Some disliked the play.

4. The recording delighted all of us.

5. The puppy looked happy.

6. Children play at the park.

7. The prize surprised him.

8. Our dinner was delicious.

9. Her aunt brought her special gifts.

10. The captain surrendered the ball.

Part Two. A preposition is always followed by its object though it may not be the very next word. In each of the following sentences, a preposition is missing its object. Put in a noun or pronoun as the missing object. Then underline the subject of the sentence *once* and the verb *twice*. The first sentence has been done as an example.

      students
11. <u>All</u> of the ^ <u><u>voted</u></u> against the added test.

12. Into the marched the excited crowd.

13. We decided to play our instruments after.

14. Neither of the wanted to be chosen captain of the team.

15. Whenever we walk over to the we encounter adventures.

16. Few children in who have behavioral problems.

17. Cooking with is quite healthy.

18. Were any of at that movie?

19. The decision of our was to cancel the next meeting.

20. Please include your resume and job history in your.

Main Verbs and Helping Verbs

Verbs can be either **main verbs** or **helping** (also called **auxiliary**) **verbs.** Main verbs are the kind of verb you have already studied. Main verbs tell what action is being performed in a sentence. For example,

I *drive* to work each day.

This restaurant *serves* Mexican food.

Helping verbs are used in combination with main verbs. They perform two major functions:

1. Helping verbs indicate shades of meaning that cannot be expressed by a main verb alone. Consider the differences in meaning in the following sentences, in which the helping verbs have been italicized.

    I *may* marry you soon.   I *must* marry you soon.
    I *should* marry you soon.   I *can* marry you soon.

As you can see, changing the helping verb changes the meaning of the entire sentence. These differences in meaning could not be expressed simply by using the main verb *marry* alone.

2.   Helping verbs also show tense—the time at which the action of the verb takes place. Notice how changing the helping verb in the following sentences helps to change the tense of the main verb *visit*. (Both the helping verbs and the main verbs have been italicized.)

He *is visiting* New York.
He *will visit* New York.
He *has visited* New York.

Notice the position that helping verbs have in a sentence. They always *come before* the main verb although sometimes another word, such as an adverb, may come between the helping verb and the main verb.

The team *can win* the game.
The team *can* probably *win* the game.
You *should stay* in bed today.
You *should* definitely *stay* in bed today.

If a question contains a helping verb, the helping verb still *comes before* the main verb.

Can the team *win* the game?
Should you *stay* in bed today?
Does the car *run* well?
When *is* the plane *departing?*

The following words are helping verbs. *Memorize them.*

can, could
may, might, must
shall, should
will, would

The following words can be used either as helping verbs or as main verbs. They are helping verbs if they are used in combination with a main verb. They are main verbs if they occur alone. *Memorize them.*

Harcourt Brace & Company

has, have, had (forms of the verb *have*)
does, do, did, done (forms of the verb *do*)
am, is, are, was, were, been (forms of the verb *be*)

As Main Verbs	*As Helping Verbs*
He *has* my book.	He *has gone* home.
She *did* a headstand.	She *did* not *arrive* on time.
We *are* hungry.	We *are eating* soon.

From now on, whenever you are asked to identify the verbs in a sentence, *include all the main verbs and all the helping verbs.* For example, in the sentence "We should review this lesson," the complete verb is "should review." In the sentence "He has lost his wallet," the verb is "has lost." Underline the complete verbs in the following sentences.

Gail must borrow some money.
I may go to Hawaii this summer.
Sheila can speak German fluently.
We are leaving soon.

Some sentences may contain more than one helping verb.

one helping verb	The mechanic *is working* on your car.
two helping verbs	He *must have lost* your phone number.
three helping verbs	That bill *should have been paid* by now.

Underline the subjects of the following sentences *once* and the complete verbs *twice.*

You could have sold your car for a better price.
The weather will be getting warmer soon.
You have not been listening to me.
Do you have a part-time job?
You should have gone to the dentist last week.
My cousin may be visiting me this summer.

Remember this rule:

The verbs in a sentence include all the main verbs plus all the helping verbs.

Underline the subjects of the following sentences *once* and the complete verbs *twice*. Some sentences may have more than one subject, more than one set of verbs, or both. Remember to cross out prepositional phrases first.

1. Many of you may like to hike up mountains and in forests.

2. People have hiked on trails for hundreds of years.

3. Hikers today might usually hike for exercise or recreation.

4. Settlers and Native Americans did not hike for exercise; they hiked to travel somewhere.

5. The Old North Trail may be the oldest and longest trail in North America.

6. This trail was created by Native Americans between the Rocky Mountains and the Great Plains, at the base of the eastern side of the Rocky Mountains.

7. The Native Americans and early settlers must have needed to travel far because the Old North Trail runs 2,000 to 3,000 miles from Canada down into Mexico.

8. This trail would be similar to an interstate highway today.

9. This trail might contradict our idea of Native Americans only protecting a certain territory.

10. The Blackfeet tribe in Canada may have traveled as far south as Mexico.

11. Many trips were made by the Blackfeet and other tribes of Native Americans.

12. In the late 1890s, a photographer by the name of McClintock was told about trips the Blackfeet made in the 1920s to Mexico.

13. Warriors could travel twenty to thirty miles each day.

14. Bands or families could go only five to seven miles each day.

15. It would have taken months to go very far!

16. By the 1900s, it would have been difficult to travel the Old North Trail because settlers had already built over part of the trail.

17. Today you can still see some evidence of the trail from piles of stone trail-markers and from stones from old campsites.

Harcourt Brace & Company

Underline the subjects of the following sentences *once* and the complete verbs *twice*. Some sentences may have more than one subject, more than one set of verbs, or both. Remember to cross out prepositional phrases first.

1. Did you know that coffee and coffeehouses have become very popular?

2. Until recently, we might have ordered a cup of coffee and might have been asked if we wanted regular or decaf.

3. Today, coffee may come in a dizzying assortment of varieties.

4. From caffé latté to iced blended mochas and cappuccinos, drinking coffee has changed considerably from the simple cup of "joe" of the near past.

5. The popularity of coffee has been increased by coffeehouses like Starbucks.

6. Starbucks' coffeehouses began in Seattle and quickly spread all over the United States.

7. While most people have gone to them for their wide varieties of coffee delights, now they can order bagels, muffins, and juices and purchase coffee mugs and other paraphernalia as well.

8. The nineties may become known as the "coffee decade."

9. Starbucks might have begun the trend, but now many other coffeehouses have sprung up.

10. Bookstore chains have opened coffee centers in their stores, and many coffeehouses have expanded to offer patrons books and magazines to read.

11. In fact, the coffeehouse has become a new place for people feeling lonely to find one another.

12. In the past, single people would often go to bars or clubs to find one another, but times have certainly changed.

13. In the nineties, people in need of companionship are sitting in coffeehouses while they wait for romance.

14. In the past, couples on their first dates would make conversation over glasses of wine.

15. Today, couples may find romance over an iced blended mocha or nonfat caffé latté with lots of foam.

16. Did you know that coffeehouses in the past offered entertainment in the form of folksingers?

17. Today, coffeehouses have continued this tradition.

18. Some still offer music, but they have also added performance artists and poetry readings.

19. Probably the most interesting new addition to coffeehouses has been the computer connection.

20. Cyber-coffeehouses have opened up in New York and Los Angeles.

21. At these coffee places, patrons are experiencing the opportunity to access the Internet and are finding companionship in a chat room as they sip delicious, honey-vanilla cappuccinos.

Part One. Construct sentences of your own using the helping verbs listed below.

1. must: _____

_____

2. should: _____

_____

3. can: _____

_____

4. was: _____

_____

5. has: _____

_____

6. will: _____

_____

Part Two. Construct a sentence for each of the following patterns. Make certain that the order of the subjects and verbs in your sentences is the same as the order in the pattern. Use as many different helping and main verbs as possible.

S = subject   HV = helping verb   MV = main verb

7. S-HV-MV: _____

8. S-MV: _____

9. S-MV-S-MV: _____

10. S-MV-MV: _____

11. S-HV-HV-MV: _____

12. S-HV-HV-HV-MV: _____

13. S-HV-MV-HV-MV: _____

14. HV-S-MV? (Notice that this pattern produces a question, not a statement.)

Underline the subjects of the following sentences *once* and the complete verbs *twice*. Some sentences may have more than one subject, more than one verb, or both.

Studies in popular culture have become a part of our daily life. Articles in local newspapers often report about current trends. These reports, however, do not only describe today's trends. They may also question these trends and reflect on their meaning.

Have you seen these kinds of articles? A local paper recently ran two articles of interest. One of these examined how people are getting piercings all over their bodies. In the past people would just pierce their ears. Today, people are piercing all parts of their bodies, from their ears to their toes.

This newspaper article did not simply describe this social trend. It tried to understand it. For example, it presented some ideas about why people might pierce their bodies. Sometimes, people pierce because it is a sign of acceptance into a social group. Lots of young people get piercings in order to distinguish themselves and to rebel against their parents. Sometimes people pierce themselves to become part of the experience of feeling like an outsider, or they may get piercings to show some kind of control over their bodies. This last reason is interesting. If people feel a lack of control over their own lives, they can at least control their own bodies. Does that idea make some sense?

Lots of curious things happen in our culture. It is a challenge to try to understand their significance. Another article in our local newspaper covered a concert by a rock group with the name Marilyn Manson. This group appeals to the dark side of its young audience. The writer described how the teenagers at the concert were dressed. They looked weird, but they all looked alike! The writer tried to make some sense out of this. Why would someone want to look different by looking like a lot of other people?

These articles describe popular trends and also try to investigate their meaning. Popular culture has become a fascinating study for a lot of people.

5

Recognizing
Singular and Plural
Subjects and Verbs

Errors in **subject-verb agreement** are among the most common grammatical mistakes. By applying the rules in this unit, you should be able to correct many of the errors in your own writing.

As you already know, a sentence must contain both a subject and a verb. Read the following two sentences. What is the grammatical difference between them?

The bank opens at ten o'clock in the morning.

The banks open at ten o'clock in the morning.

In the first sentence, the subject *bank* is singular. **Singular** means "one." There is *one* bank in the first sentence. In the second sentence, the subject *banks* is plural. **Plural** means "two or more." There are at least two (and possible more than two) banks in the second sentence.

Like the subject *bank,* the verb *opens* in the first sentence is singular. Verb forms ending in *-s* are used with *singular* subjects, as in the sentence "The bank *opens* at ten o'clock in the morning." The verb *open* in the second sentence above

Harcourt Brace & Company

is **plural.** This verb form (without a final -*s*) is used with *plural* subjects, as in the sentence "The banks *open* at ten o'clock in the morning."

In other words, if the subject of a sentence is *singular,* the verb in the sentence must also be *singular.* If the subject of the sentence is *plural,* the verb must be *plural.* This matching of singular subjects with singular verbs and plural subjects with plural verbs is called **subject-verb agreement.**

In order to avoid making mistakes in subject-verb agreement, you must be able to recognize the difference between singular and plural subjects and verbs.

The subjects of sentences are usually nouns or pronouns. As you know, the plurals of nouns are usually formed by adding an -*s* to singular forms.

Singular	*Plural*
envelope	envelopes
restaurant	restaurants

However, a few nouns (under 1 percent) have irregular plural forms.

Singular	*Plural*
man	men
leaf	leaves
child	children
thesis	theses
self	selves
medium	media (as in the "mass media")

Those pronouns that can be used as subjects are also singular or plural, depending upon whether they refer to one or more than one person or thing.

Singular	*Plural*
I	we
you	you
he, she, it	they

Notice that the pronoun *you* may be either singular or plural.

If nouns show number by adding -*s* to the plural, what do verbs do to show whether they are singular or plural? A long time ago English verbs had many different endings for this purpose, but most of those endings have been dropped. Today most English verbs look the same whether the subject is singular or plural: "I talk," "we talk," "the men talk," "I remembered," "they remembered," "the class remembered," and so on. However, there is one place where English verbs have kept a special ending to show number. That special ending is also an -*s*, and

the place it is added is in the **present-tense singular** with the subject pronouns *he, she, it* and with any singular noun that could replace any of these pronouns. Look at these sentences in the present tense, and notice when the *-s* is added to the verb:

Singular	*Plural*
I talk.	We talk.
You talk.	You talk.
He talks.	They talk.
She talks.	They talk.
It talks.	They talk.
The man talks.	The men talk.
The girl talks.	The girls talk.

To sum up, although adding an *-s* to most nouns (99 percent) makes them plural, some singular verbs also end with an *-s*. An easy way to remember this difference is to memorize this rule:

Any verb ending in -s is singular.

There are no exceptions to this rule. Therefore, it is not **good usage** in college writing to have a sentence in which a plural subject is matched with a verb ending in *-s*.

Effective writers are as aware of **usage** as they are of grammar. Good usage means choosing different kinds of language for different situations, just as we choose different clothes for different situations. In **informal** situations, such as conversations with friends, it is common to choose informal usage. However, almost all of the writing you do for college is in **formal** situations, such as exams and essay assignments. The difference between formal and informal usage can be seen when we make subjects agree with their verbs. Because most conversation is very informal, you may have heard or have used many informal verb choices in your own conversations. Notice the differences in usage in these examples:

Informal	*Formal*
We was here.	We were here.
He don't come here.	He doesn't come here.
They was at the beach.	They were at the beach.

You want your college writing to be as effective as you can make it. In college you must choose **formal usage** in almost every situation—essays, reports, exams, and so on. The exercises in our text are *always* designed for you to choose formal usage.

Harcourt Brace & Company

In order to avoid subject-verb agreement errors, there are some rules that you should keep in mind. (How you "keep rules in mind" is up to you. If you find that even after you study rules, you still cannot remember them, you should *memorize* the rules in this unit.)

Rule 1. A verb agrees with the subject, not with the complement. A **complement** is a word that refers to the same person or thing as the subject of the sentence. It follows a linking verb.

S   LV   C

Our main economic *problem is* rising prices.

In the sentence above, the subject is *problem,* which is singular. The subject is not *prices.* Rather, *prices* is the complement. Therefore, the linking verb takes the singular form *is* to agree with *problem.* If the sentence is reversed, it reads:

S   LV   C

Rising *prices are* our main economic problem.

The subject is now the plural noun *prices,* and *problem* is the complement. The verb now takes the plural form *are.* Which are the correct verbs in the following sentences?

The topic of discussion (was, were) political refugees.

Astrological signs (seems, seem) to be an interesting subject to many people.

Rule 2. Prepositional phrases have no effect on a verb.

The *president,* with his chief economic advisors, *is having* a press conference today.

In the sentence above, the subject is singular (*president*). The prepositional phrase, *with his chief economic advisors,* has no effect on the verb, which remains singular (*is having*).

A *hamburger* with french fries *costs* two dollars.

The singular verb *costs* agrees with the singular subject *hamburger.* The prepositional phrase *with french fries* has no effect on the verb. Which is the correct verb in the following sentence?

Harcourt Brace & Company

The woman with her ten cats (was, were) evicted for breaking the clause in her lease which prohibited the keeping of pets.

In addition, do not mistakenly make your verb agree with a noun or pronoun in a prepositional phrase. (This is easy to do because many prepositional phrases come just before a verb.)

The *problems* of this school district *trouble* the school board greatly.

In the sentence above, the subject is plural (*problems*). The plural verb *trouble* agrees with *problems*, not with the singular object of the preposition (*district*).

The attitude of adolescents is often difficult to understand.

The singular verb *is* agrees with the singular subject *attitude*, not with the plural object of the preposition (*adolescents*).

Which are the correct verbs in the following sentences?

One of the restaurants (serves, serve) Thai food. The directions for the test (was, were) confusing.

Rule 3. Be especially alert for subject-verb agreement when the sentence has **inverted word order** as in these three situations:

a) **Questions**

Notice the location of the subject in these questions:

HV S MV
Does he want a new car? (subject between helping and main verb)

V   S
Is turkey your favorite food? (subject after main verb)

Interrogative words like *when, where,* and *how* come at the beginning of sentence patterns, but they are never subjects.

HV   S   MV
When *does* the game *start?* (subject between helping and main verb)

```
        MV    S
```
Where *is* the *picnic?* (subject after verb)

```
       HV  S  MV
```
How *can he study* all weekend? (subject between helping and main verb)

b) Sentence patterns beginning with *here* or *there*

The words *here* and *there* are never subjects.
Notice the location of the subject in these patterns:

There *are* many *children* here today. (subject after verb)

Here *are* your test *results.* (subject after verb)

c) Rare patterns in which the verb precedes the subject

Occasionally a writer will, for emphasis, put a subject after its verb.
Notice the location of the subject in these sentences:

Behind the lamp in the corner *was* the very expensive *statue.* (If the order of this sentence were reversed, it would read, "The very expensive statue was behind the lamp in the corner.")

Toward the finish line *raced* the breathless *runner.* ("The breathless runner raced toward the finish line.")

Circle the verb that correctly completes each sentence. Make certain that you have identified the correct subject of the sentence and that you have crossed out prepositional phrases.

1. Shakespeare's plays (continues, continue) to enchant people of all ages.

2. The plays for most people (is, are) difficult to read.

3. Yet, there (is, are) several sure signs pointing to Shakespeare's amazing popularity.

4. In most homes, a collection of Shakespeare's plays rarely (finds, find) prominence over magazines or newspapers.

5. Nonetheless, there (is, are) few of us who don't know about *Romeo and Juliet.*

6. Why (does, do) the plays of Shakespeare so engage us?

7. Just during the 1990s so many movies of Shakespeare (was, were) made.

8. One of these films (was, were) Kenneth Branagh's *Much Ado About Nothing.*

9. Among other popular Shakespeare films (was, were) Mel Gibson's *Hamlet.*

10. Then there (was, were) all of those films about Richard III.

11. However, of all the stories of Shakespeare, *Romeo and Juliet* no doubt (is, are) loved the most.

12. The most recent film version of this great love story (takes, take) place in a current time period with rap music!

13. So much of the audience for this film (seems, seem) to be quite young.

Harcourt Brace & Company

14. The stories of Shakespeare (touches, touch) a universal chord in all of us, no matter what our age.

15. His fascinating characters (is, are) one of the reasons for the continuing popularity of his plays.

16. The artistry of this great playwright (has, have) no time or age barriers.

Some of the sentences in this exercise contain subject-verb agreement errors. Others are correct as written. If the sentence contains a subject-verb agreement error, cross out the incorrect verb, and write the correct verb in its place. If the sentence is *correct,* write a *C* in the left margin.

1. Do you think only boys join gangs?

2. Well, sometimes, girls joins gangs.

3. There is many reasons why they join.

4. The influences of family structure has proved to be an important area explaining why girls involve themselves in gangs.

5. Parents often has little control over their daughters and cannot prevent their daughters from associating with gang members.

6. In addition, problems within a family sometimes causes girls to join gangs.

7. In fact, an important reason for joining gangs given by girls are the importance of belonging to a family-like group.

8. But while the need to be part of a group bring girls to gangs, so does other factors.

9. Some girls says they joins gangs simply because gangs are part of their environment.

10. They needs gangs for self-protection.

11. Interestingly, the most profound reason girls offer for joining a gang is revenge.

12. Their reason for joining gangs are to get back at someone who has hurt either them or a loved one.

13. Gang identity hold importance to girls involved in gangs.

14. To remain in a gang, a girl have to "back up" (defend) her neighborhood at all times.

15. The names of some gangs comes from a street or city while others may have a name referring to an age group.

16. For example, the name of one of Los Angeles's many gangs are "Tiny Locas" (Tiny Crazies) because the girls are young.

17. One of the worst characteristics of life in a gang for girls are violence.

18. A gang use violence in order to "jump in" (initiate) a girl who wants to become part of the gang.

19. Violence also become a way the gang members protect their neighborhood.

20. Sadly, many young girls loses their lives in gang wars.

21. Growing up today has certainly become a more difficult and complicated matter.

In the following sentences, change each plural subject to its singular form and change each singular subject to its plural form. As you change each subject, change its verb to agree with it. You may also have to add or delete the indefinite articles *a* and *an*. The first sentence has been done as an example.

A dog guards
1. ~~Dogs guard~~ the junkyard.

2. Have the singers arrived on stage yet?

3. The books on that desk need to be delivered.

4. Here is the report.

5. There were important reasons for the disaster.

6. Does the kitten have enough milk?

7. The intelligent child in that classroom plays the piano very well.

8. The athletes need more practice.

9. The person with a strong will and discipline tends to succeed.

10. Do the coaches consider all the possible plays?

11. The actor reads the speech quite well.

12. The piano in the den needs to be tuned again.

13. Teachers in a high school usually have five years of college education.

14. During the rainy season, the street around the bend from us floods a great deal.

15. Certain pictures in the museum attract lots of attention.

16. In a special gallery of the museum is a rare painting by Rembrandt.

17. The young boy looks sad today.

18. The video games have become very popular.

19. A computer game sometimes comes with a code book.

20. Do the code books help the players to reach higher levels of the games?

Indefinite Pronouns as Subjects

The subject pronouns we have been studying, like *she* or *it* or *they,* refer to specific, definite persons or things. This chapter is about another kind of pronoun, **indefinite pronouns,** which do not refer to a specific person or to definite things.

Rule 4. The following indefinite pronouns are **singular** and require **singular** verbs:

anybody, anyone, anything

each, each one

either, neither

everybody, everyone, everything

nobody, no one, nothing

somebody, someone, something

Harcourt Brace & Company

Everybody has his camping gear.

Anything goes.

Each of the players *knows* the ground rules.

Either of those times *is* all right with me.

Notice that in the last two sentences, the verbs agree with the singular subjects *each* and *either.* The verbs are not affected by the plural nouns in the prepositional phrases *of these players* or *of those times.*

Rule 5. Indefinite pronouns, such as the words *some, half, most,* and *all,* may take either singular or plural verbs, depending upon their meaning in the context of the sentence. If these words tell **how much** of something is meant, the verb is singular; but if they tell **how many** of something is meant, the verb is plural.

Most of the milk *is* stale. (how much?)

Most of the actors *are* present. (how many?)

Some of the butter *is* missing. (how much?)

Some of the players *were* late. (how many?)

All of the fortune *goes* to the family. (how much?)

All of these items *go* to us. (how many?)

Do not confuse the words in this rule with the words *each, either,* and *neither* in Rule 4. These three words *always* require a singular verb.

Harcourt Brace & Company

Circle the verb that correctly completes each sentence. This exercise covers only the rules from Lesson 6.

1. All of those clothes (belongs, belong) to them.

2. Some of the stores on this street (sells, sell) exotic items.

3. Each of the characters in the play (reflects, reflect) a cultural trait.

4. Most of the milk (was, were) spilled.

5. Some of the cars (is, are) parked illegally.

6. No one of the team's members (knows, know) the correct rules.

7. Nothing we do (seems, seem) to go right.

8. (Is, Are) anybody keeping score?

9. Most of the team (practices, practice) daily.

10. Neither of the candidates (speaks, speak) eloquently.

This part of the exercise covers rules from Lessons 5 and 6.

11. Here (is, are) the new rules.

12. Chocolate cake with ice cream (makes, make) a good dessert.

13. The rumors about the teachers (is, are) false.

14. Here (comes, come) the bride!

15. Around the corner and under the car (hides, hide) the puppies.

16. (Does, do) the store's workers truly get raises?

17. Some of the buildings (needs, need) refurbishing.

18. Most of the actors (loves, love) the craft of acting.

19. The salesman (produces, produce) a significant amount of business.

20. There (was, were) giggles in the audience.

Some of the sentences in this exercise contain subject-verb agreement errors. Others are correct as written. If the sentence contains a subject-verb agreement error, cross out the incorrect verb and write the correct verb in its place. If the sentence is *correct,* write a *C* in the margin by the sentence number. This exercise covers rules from Lesson 5 and 6.

1. No one seem to understand the problem.

2. Neither side argues the issues well.

3. Most of the people appreciates the complications of the situation.

4. Somebody in these classes have lost three tickets.

5. Each boy wears the class sweater at the reception.

6. Most of the milk was gone.

7. All of the flowers is blooming now.

8. Everybody knows how much time it takes to clean a house.

9. If no one at this time answer the door, just move along.

10. At least half of the participants considers the lectures very informative.

11. There was many reasons why the house sold so quickly.

12. At what time does the members of the team arrive?

13. Is it true that most of our natural resources are dwindling?

14. All of the soda were drunk by the little children.

15. Some of the wheat are still left in that bin.

16. Neither of the teams have won any prizes yet.

17. Something seem strange here!

18. The reasons for all that commotion is very clear.

19. Despite our best efforts, most of the work still need to be done.

20. There was simply too many of us at the party.

Part One. In the following sentences, change all the singular subjects to their plural form and all the plural subjects to their singular form. If these changes affect subject-verb agreement, then change the verb to match the new subject. You may also have to add or delete the indefinite articles *a* and *an*. The first sentence has been done as an example.

A club meets
1. ~~Clubs meets~~ here often.

2. The politician is in the next room.

3. Where have your friends gone?

4. The reporter often speaks to our class.

5. There are your best sketches behind the sofa.

6. Does the artist perform at the club we attend?

7. The guitar player accompanies the singer.

8. The children play often at our house.

Part Two. Complete each sentence by adding an appropriate prepositional phrase beginning with *of*. Make certain that the prepositional phrase you add does not affect the verb. Sentence 9 has been done as an example.

of the girls
9. All ^ are here.

10. Neither wants to work.

11. Most love the book.

12. Each plays his part well.

13. Half was eaten.

14. Some were sold to the army.

15. Either makes me happy.

Part Three. Complete each sentence by adding an appropriate present-tense verb. Sentence 16 has been done as an example.

16. No one *likes* to lose.

17. Each of the children _____ a new toy.

18. Everyone _____ a good laugh.

19. Neither of the candidates _____ a tax cut.

20. Somebody _____ beautiful pictures.

21. Everybody _____ Dr. Martin Luther King's beautiful speech "I Have a Dream."

22. Officially, the twenty-first century _____ in the year 2001, not in 2000.

Subjects Understood in a Special Sense

This chapter discusses as subjects several small groups of words that call for special attention in subject-verb agreement.

Rule 6. Some subjects, though **plural in form,** are **singular in meaning** and, therefore, require a singular verb. Such words include *news, mathematics, physics, economics, aeronautics, electronics, molasses, mumps,* and *measles.*

Economics was my least favorite class.

Mumps is a common disease among children.

Rule 7. A unit of time, weight, measurement, or **money** usually requires a singular verb because the entire amount is thought of as a single unit.

Twenty *dollars is* all the money I have.

Two *pounds* of meat *feeds* four people.

Eighteen *yards* of cloth *completes* our fabric needs.

Rule 8. Collective nouns usually require singular verbs. A collective noun is a word that is singular in form but that refers to a group of people or things. Some common collective nouns are words such as *group, team, family, class, crowd,* and *committee.*

The *crowd is* very noisy.

The *committee holds* frequent meetings.

Occasionally, a collective noun may be used with a plural verb if the writer wishes to show that the members of the group are acting as separate individuals rather than as a unified body. Notice the difference in meaning between the following pair of sentences:

The *Board of Directors supports* the measure. (In this sentence, the *Board of Directors* is acting as a single, unified group.)

The *Board of Directors are divided* over whether to pass the measure. (In this sentence, the *Board of Directors* is viewed as a collection of separate individuals who, because they are not in agreement, are not acting as a unified group.)

Circle the verb that correctly completes each sentence. This section of the exercise covers only the rules in Lesson 7.

1. The team (goes, go) to Dallas each weekend.

2. Our family (agrees, agree) on just about everything.

3. One thousand dollars (seems, seem) a lot of money for a dress.

4. The mumps (is, are) one illness I don't want to get.

5. Thirty minutes (is, are) just enough time to do my situps.

6. Electronics (appears, appear) to be a growing field of study.

7. The crowd joyfully (cheers, cheer) the candidate.

8. (Is, are) the news on now?

9. Politics (gives, give) me lots of things to discuss.

10. The class (claps, clap) after every lecture.

The following sentences cover rules from Lessons 5–7.

11. All of the land (seems, seem) to be arid.

12. Each of the play's characters (responds, respond) with passion to the situation.

13. In the middle of the desert (grows, grow) beautiful flowers.

14. One of the issues to be discussed (is, are) the future of our club.

15. Most of the class (participates, participate) in the discussions.

16. (Does, Do) some of your family play instruments?

17. In the center of her room (sit, sits) thirteen stuffed animals.

18. Here (rests, rest) several exhausted gymnasts.

19. There (hasn't, haven't) been many calls today.

20. Everyone (wishes, wish) for a bright future.

Harcourt Brace & Company

Some of the sentences in this exercise contain one or more subject-verb agreement errors. Others are correct as written. If the sentence contains a subject-verb agreement error, cross out the incorrect verb, and write the *correct* form in its place. If the sentence is correct, write a *C* in the left margin. This exercise covers rules from Lessons 5–7.

1. Some groups of citizens feels that music for young people need to be policed.

2. There has been, in fact, a successful movement to put parental advisory labels on recordings.

3. Of all the kinds of music that young people listen to, one of the most controversial types have probably been rap music.

4. Do anyone think that rap music is too violent and even sexist—saying unkind things about women?

5. Some groups believes this is the truth.

6. For example, the news often have reports about rappers in trouble with the law.

7. There has been several songs that suggests lawlessness.

8. Many of the critics points to Ice T's "Cop Killer" as an example.

9. Most parents takes offense even at the title of 2 Live Crew's album *Nasty As They Wanna Be.*

10. Many listeners agrees that the lyrics in this album is sexually explicit and obscene.

11. In "Cop Killer," the lyrics centers around the assassination of police.

12. What does rappers say in response to these criticisms?

13. Rappers contend that their music is a valid form of expression with lyrics simply telling it as it is.

14. Some of these songwriters even argues that if they try to rap about non-violent topics, they won't get contracts.

15. But proponents of rap says that there is some "serious" rappers.

16. There are female rappers who rap about serious and important issues.

17. But other critics contend that most of the rap performers influences kids in negative ways.

18. Rap music bring up a very serious issue.

19. Do a group of people have the right to censor or limit any form of expression if it is very controversial?

20. Issues of this kind provokes intense debates among students of the First Amendment.

21. Are the United States a place where open discussion on any subject can occur?

Some of the sentences in this exercise contain subject-verb agreement errors. Others are correct as written. If the sentence contains a subject-verb agreement error, cross out the incorrect verb, and write the correct form in its place. If the sentence is *correct,* write *C* in the left margin. This exercise covers rules from Lessons 5–8.

1. Physics confuses me.

2. Everyone at the summer games were delighted.

3. Some of the milk has spoiled.

4. The committee agree on the outcome.

5. The news today is shocking.

6. Marisa says that mathematics are her best subject.

7. Ryan and Kathy thought molasses were a great food treat.

8. Ben knew that twenty miles are too far to travel in a storm.

9. Neither of the stores sell organic fruits and vegetables.

10. A cup of coffee with a doughnut cost a dollar.

11. Where is most of the committee members today?

12. Health spas is a favorite vacation spot for wealthy people.

13. Three yards of rope aren't enough for this job.

14. Most of the food is gone now.

Harcourt Brace & Company

15. Either of those remarks hurt my feelings.

16. Some of the class resents the announcement.

17. All of his time is spent practicing the guitar.

18. Everyone of us delight in his presence.

8

Subjects Joined by Conjunctions

Subjects joined by conjunctions require the special rules in this chapter.

Rule 9. Two subjects joined by the conjunction *and* are plural and require a plural verb.

French and *Italian are* both Romance languages.

UCLA and *USC* both *have* excellent film schools.

Rule 10. When *each, every,* or *any* is used as an adjective in front of subjects, the subjects that are modified require a singular verb. (Writers have the most trouble with this rule when the sentence has two or more subjects joined by *and,* so this rule is an exception to Rule 9, above.)

Each boy and girl under the age of five *rides* the bus free of charge.

Every Tom, Dick, and Harry *wants* to borrow money from me.

Harcourt Brace & Company

Notice that the adjectives *every* and *each* make the verbs in the sentences singular even though each sentence has more than one subject.

Rule 11. Two singular subjects joined by the conjunctions *or* or *nor* are singular and require a singular verb.

Neither *John* nor *Harold knows* the telephone number.

Monday or *Tuesday is* my parents' anniversary.

Rule 12. If both a singular and a plural subject are joined by *or* or *nor,* the subject that is *closer* to the verb determines whether the verb is singular or plural.

Either two *onions* or a *clove* of garlic *is* necessary for this recipe.

Either a *clove* of garlic or two *onions are* necessary for this recipe.

Is a *clove* of garlic or two *onions* necessary for this recipe?

Are two *onions* or a *clove* of garlic necessary for this recipe?

(Note: In the final two sentences, it is the *helping* verb that agrees with the subject.)

Circle the verb that correctly completes each sentence. This section of the exercise covers only the rules in Lesson 8.

1. Students and professors (enjoys, enjoy) discussions over coffee.

2. Each player, manager, and fan (wants, want) the games to go on.

3. Neither the store owner nor her employees (understands, understand) the problem.

4. Either soup or salad (is, are) our choice for lunch.

5. Either the doctor or the nurses (takes, take) your temperature.

6. Pagers and cellular phones (has, have) become quite popular.

7. (Is, Are) a pager or a cellular phone on your Christmas list?

8. Rosemary chicken and potatoes (is, are) the traditional Christmas meal in England.

9. Every senator and congressman (belongs, belong) to a committee.

10. Neither the producer nor the writers (likes, like) the show.

This section covers rules from Lessons 6–9.

11. (Has, Have) the orchestra tuned up yet?

12. In the middle of the orchestra pit (stands, stand) the conductor.

13. Here (is, are) the ingredients for the cake.

14. Some of his hobbies (includes, include) fishing and swimming.

15. Most of the soccer players (comes, come) from outside the United States.

16. The jury (has, have) deliberated for a considerable time now.

17. Music (is, are) one of my favorite subjects.

18. Only the judge or the jury foreman (sees, see) the verdict.

19. Either the district attorney or the defendants (is, are) going to be happy.

20. Central to this case (is, are) eyewitness accounts.

Some of the sentences in this exercise contain subject-verb agreement errors. Others are correct as written. If the sentence contains a subject-verb agreement error, cross out the incorrect verb, and write the correct form in its place. If the sentence is *correct,* write *C* in the left margin. This exercise covers rules from Lessons 5–8.

1. Popular music certainly play a large part in our lives.

2. In some ways, popular music and popular performers reflects the spirit of the times.

3. Neither the Beatles nor Bob Dylan individually represent the sixties, but together they do tell us something about that time period.

4. Each performer and his music embody a piece of the historical moment.

5. For example, the antiwar songs of Bob Dylan captures the feeling of the late sixties and early seventies.

6. Groups like the Grateful Dead, on the other hand, reflects a less political and more playful characteristic of that period.

7. In some ways, our reviews or assessment of past periods are a lot easier to make than to understand what is actually occurring in the present.

8. Because the nineties presents us with a more diversified field of popular music than did the sixties, finding one theme isn't easy.

9. In fact, the generation of the nineties were given the name "Generation X" partly because a true or singular identity couldn't be found.

10. Each generation and its leaders looks to find a way to express itself against earlier generations.

11. The nineties' "Generation X" embraces all kinds of music.

12. One kind of music that continues to be popular are heavy metal music.

Harcourt Brace & Company

13. Metallica are a band that began in the eighties and continue to be popular into the nineties.

14. Neither their music nor their lyrics is peaceful, gentle, or playful.

15. The title of their first album tell it all: *Kill 'em All!*

16. Songs like "No Remorse," "Seek and Destroy," and "Am I Evil?" suggests how angry and disillusioned both the singers and their audience are.

17. In the song "Justice for All," the words "I can't believe the things you say/ I can't believe" clearly communicate the cynicism and disillusionment felt by many in both the late eighties and nineties.

18. While music of the sixties generally preached peace, love, and revolution, neither the music nor the performers of the nineties suggests a belief in anything even close to such things.

Some of the sentences in this exercise contain subject-verb agreement errors. Others are correct as written. If a sentence contains a subject-verb agreement error, cross out the incorrect verb, and write the correct verb in its place. If a sentence is *correct,* write *C* in the left margin. This exercise covers the rules in Lessons 5–8.

1. Probably everyone watch television every day.

2. Most of the viewers thinks of television as entertainment.

3. Some people, however, sees it only as a vehicle for information.

4. Neither entertainment nor information completely capture the range of television in our lives.

5. Certainly there is some shows that both entertain and inform.

6. But now television writers has created a new type of show.

7. This type of program combines both entertainment and information.

8. Some of these shows looks like magazines on television.

9. Each of the shows have several different stories.

10. Each story and segment have a different producer and writer, just like the stories in a magazine.

11. A good example of such a show are one you know very well.

12. Most of us has watched *Entertainment Tonight,* a very long-running and successful magazine show.

13. Another kind of television program combining entertainment and information is "reality TV."

14. Viewers still enjoys *Rescue 911,* a good example of this kind of program.

15. But some of these new reality programs is a bit confusing.

16. Each of us viewers have expectations about what a show means.

17. For example, we believe that the "news" is real and dramatic shows are fictional.

18. *Rescue 911* and other shows like it changes everything.

19. Suddenly, fiction and reality is brought together in one show.

20. Everyone certainly thinks he or she know the difference between reality and fiction.

21. But in these shows, such distinctions seems to disappear.

Correct any subject-verb agreement errors that you find in the following essay by crossing out the incorrect verb and writing in the correct form. It may help you to underline all the subjects in the essay *once* and all the verbs *twice* before you try to identify errors in agreement.

American tall tales is one of my favorite kinds of story. The crazy, off-the-wall exaggerations is what I like the most about these stories. Two folk tales that I like a lot is "Paul Bunyan" and "John Henry." Each of these stories of American legends fill me with wonder and laughter.

The story of John Henry really do two things. First, it tells about a very strong and wonderful man, and second, it comment on the way the Industrial Age was changing American lives. In this legend, John Henry, an ex-slave, discover his talent in life: to work on the railroad as a steel-driving man. Of all the hardworking men in all of the country working on the railroad, the hardest-working man of all are John Henry. Then, along come a man with amazing machines and challenge John Henry to a match. John Henry beats the machines, but he die from his efforts. It is sad because John Henry know that the machines will ultimately take over.

Probably Paul Bunyan provide us with some of the most fantastic tall tales. One of my favorites are the one about the bunkhouse he have to build for his workers. This bunkhouse is so tall that each of the men have to ride a hot air balloon to get to his bunk; to come down they parachutes! Even more astounding is the story of the corn he plants. This plant grow so fast that the worker who is climbing it to collect the corn can't come down. Paul Bunyan shoot biscuits to him so he won't starve. Finally, the plant grow so tall that it reaches the sun. The heat of the sun turn the corn into popcorn, and the sky rain popcorn all over the place. A herd of cattle think this popcorn rain is a snowstorm, and all of them freezes to death!

These stories are pretty silly, but they're lots of fun.

Harcourt Brace & Company

Correct all the subject-verb agreement errors you find in the following paragraphs.

Languedoc (lahng-DOC) is a region in southern France. Among its most famous dishes are a casserole called a *cassoulet* [cæh-soo-LAY]. The basis of this dish are dried white beans. Pieces of roast duck gives the casserole a rich flavor. Pork or lamb are often added, and most of the recipes for cassoulet also includes sausage. As you can see, neither calories nor cholesterol are a concern of people who eat this rich dish.

Preparing a cassoulet is very time-consuming. Each of the main ingredients require advance preparation before the cassoulet as a whole is assembled. For example, almost two hours are needed just to precook the beans. In addition, every piece of meat and poultry need to be precooked too. The duck must be broiled, and the pork and lamb has to be cut in pieces and browned. Either garlic or onions is needed for seasoning and must be chopped and sautéed in the fat from the cooked meat. Parsley, along with small amounts of bay leaves and leeks, provide additional seasoning. Two cups of

Harcourt Brace & Company

peeled, seeded, and chopped tomatoes add liquid to the recipe; the rest of the liquid come from white wine and from the chicken stock used to cook the beans.

The cassoulet is assembled in layers in a deep baking dish. Either beans or meat are in each of the layers. A topping of bread crumbs are spread over the top layer, and the cassoulet is put into the oven to bake for an hour or more. However, there are still an additional series of steps in the preparation of the dish. After the layer of crumbs have formed a firm brown crust, the crust is pushed back into the casserole, and the cassoulet is baked some more until a new crust has formed. This process can be repeated several more times. Each of the layers of crust add flavor and texture to the cassoulet.

The finished cassoulet is delicious and makes an unforgettable meal, but time and patience is definitely needed to prepare this recipe.

Harcourt Brace & Company

IDENTIFYING AND PUNCTUATING THE MAIN TYPES OF SENTENCES

Compound Sentences

A **compound sentence,** a very common sentence pattern, contains *at least two subjects and two verbs,* usually arranged in an S-V/S-V pattern. For example,

    S   V   S   V
Bob wrecked his car last week, and now he rides the bus to work.

    S   V   S   V
Nina lived in Italy for two years, so she speaks Italian fluently.

In grammar, the term **compound** means "having two or more parts." Thus, a sentence may have a **compound subject;** for example, "The *husband* and his *wife* were at the opera." Or, a sentence may have a **compound verb;** for example, "The man *rode* his bike and *sped* down the street." Do not confuse a sentence with a **compound subject** or a **compound verb** with a **compound sentence.**

A compound sentence can be divided into two parts, each of which can be a separate sentence by itself.

Bob wrecked his car last week.

    +

Now he rides the bus to work.

Nina lived in Italy for two years.

    +

She speaks Italian very fluently.

Since a compound sentence can be divided into *two* separate sentences, each half of a compound sentence must contain at least one subject and one verb. Therefore, each half of a compound sentence is a **clause.** A clause is a group of words that contains both a subject and a verb. (In contrast, a group of words that does not contain both a subject and a verb is called a **phrase,** as in a prepositional phrase.) A clause that can stand alone as a complete sentence is called an **independent clause.** Since each clause in a compound sentence can stand alone as a complete sentence, each clause must be independent. In other words,

A compound sentence consists of at least two independent clauses joined together to form a single sentence.

There are two ways to join independent clauses in order to form a compound sentence. The most frequently used method is to put a conjunction between the clauses. A **conjunction** is a word that joins words or groups of words. In grammar, the word *coordinate* means "of equal importance." Therefore, the conjunctions that are used in compound sentences are called **coordinating conjunctions** because they join two groups of words that are of equal grammatical importance. (They are both independent clauses.) The following coordinating conjunctions are used to join the clauses of compound sentences:

and

but

for (when it means *because*)

or

Harcourt Brace & Company

90

so

yet

You should *memorize* these coordinating conjunctions because later you will have to be able to distinguish between them and the connecting words that are used to form other kinds of sentences.

In the following sentences, underline the subjects of the compound sentences *once* and the verbs *twice,* and circle the coordinating conjunction that joins the clauses. Notice that a comma *precedes* the coordinating conjunction.

The president entered the room, and the band began to play "Hail to the Chief."

She diets constantly, but her weight remains the same.

I rarely prepare casseroles, for my family refuses to eat them.

We must hurry, or we will miss the first part of the movie.

He can't help you, nor can I.

(Notice that when the conjunction *nor* is used to join two independent clauses, the pattern becomes S-V/V-S: My coat isn't here, nor is my hat.)

The defendant was ill, so the trial was postponed.

He earns only eight hundred dollars a month, yet he lives quite comfortably.

Construct compound sentences of your own, using the coordinating conjunctions listed below to join your clauses. Underline the subject of each clause *once* and the verb *twice.* (You may construct a clause that has more than one subject and/or more than one verb, but each clause must have *at least* one subject and one verb.)

_____, and _____

_____, but _____

_____, for _____

_____, or _____

The second way to join the clauses in a compound sentence is to use a semicolon (;) *in place of both the comma and the coordinating conjunction.* For example,

She could not find her keys; they must have fallen somewhere.

Mark is always late for work; he oversleeps every morning.

Compound sentences constructed with semicolons occur less frequently than compound sentences constructed with coordinating conjunctions because some type of connecting word is usually needed to show the relationship between the clauses. For example, without a coordinating conjunction the logical relationship between the two clauses in the following sentence might be confusing.

My grandfather has lived in the United States for fifty years; he has never learned to speak English.

If, however, you replace the semicolon with a coordinating conjunction, the relationship between the clauses becomes clear.

My grandfather has lived in the United States for fifty years, but he has never learned to speak English.

It is all right to use the semicolon by itself between the clauses of a compound sentence, but do so only when the relationship between the clauses is clear without a connecting word.

Construct two compound sentences of your own, using semicolons to join the clauses. Underline the subjects *once* and the verbs *twice*. Make certain that each clause has at least one subject and one verb.

_____; _____;

_____; _____;

Another common way to show the relationship between the clauses of a compound sentence is to use a **conjunctive adverb,** like *however,* in the second clause. Notice that a *semicolon* is required between the clauses. A comma follows the conjunctive adverb.

We all studied quite hard; however, the test was more difficult than we had expected.

Conjunctive adverbs are especially frequent in formal language where expressing the precise relationship between ideas is the goal. Here are the most frequently used conjunctive adverbs:

Harcourt Brace & Company

also	incidentally	nonetheless
anyway	indeed	otherwise
besides	instead	still
consequently	likewise	then
finally	meanwhile	therefore
furthermore	moreover	thus
hence	nevertheless	
however	next	

A conjunctive adverb gets its double name from the fact that it does two things at once: it connects, like other **conjunctions,** and it modifies, like other **adverbs.** Because it is adverbial, it can be located in many places in its own clause. And because it can move around in the second clause and does not always come *exactly between* the two clauses (like coordinating conjunctions), it does not necessarily act as a signal to readers that they are coming to the second half of a compound sentence. For these reasons, the strong signal of a semicolon marks the end of the first clause.

Bob loved to surf; therefore, he lived near the beach.

Bob loved to surf; he, therefore, lived near the beach.

Bob loved to surf; he lived near the beach, therefore.

Roberto drives carefully; his brother, however, does not.

(Notice that the conjunctive adverb is always "set off" with a comma, or two commas, in its own clause.) Construct three compound sentences of your own that use conjunctive adverbs. Try putting the conjunctive adverb in several different places in the second clause.

1. _____

_____

2. _____

_____

3. _____

_____

(Did you remember to "set off" the conjunctive adverb with one or two commas?)

As you can see from the sentences that you have constructed in this lesson, the following punctuation rules apply to compound sentences:

1. If the clauses in a compound sentence are joined by a coordinating conjunction, place a comma *before* (to the left of) the conjunction.

This sentence is compound, *and* it contains a comma.

You may have learned that it is not necessary to use commas in short compound sentences (for example, "He's a Scorpio and I'm a Libra."). Although this is true, not everyone agrees on how short a "short" compound sentence is, so if you are in doubt, it is safer to use a comma. All the sentences in the exercises for this unit will be "long" compound sentences and should have a comma before the conjunction.

2. Although a compound sentence may contain more than one coordinating conjunction, the comma is placed before the conjunction that joins the clauses.

Jan *and* I attended the same college, *and* now we work for the same company.

3. If the clauses in a compound sentence are *not* joined by a coordinating conjunction, place a semicolon between the clauses.

I don't have my book with me; I must have left it at home.

We hurried to the theater; however, the film was over.

This sentence has two independent clauses; it is, therefore, a compound sentence.

The following sentence patterns do *not* require commas because they are **simple** (meaning that they contain only one clause) rather than compound.

S-V-V	He ordered a baked potato but was served french fries instead. (no comma)
S-S-V	My uncle and aunt live in Boston. (no comma)
S-S-V-V	My cousin and I went to England and stayed there for two months. (no comma)

To review, the two patterns for punctuating a compound sentence are:

clause + comma + coordinating conjunction + clause

We went to a play, and next we had some dinner.

clause + semicolon + clause

We went to a play; next we had some dinner.

I love to draw; however, I have little artistic talent.

Harcourt Brace & Company

Make each of the following independent clauses a compound sentence by adding
an appropriate coordinating conjunction and a second independent clause. Try to
use as many different conjunctions in this exercise as possible. Remember to
place a comma before the coordinating conjunction.

1. I want my boss to give me a raise _____

_____

2. All the tickets to the concert have been sold _____

_____

3. The results of the election haven't been announced yet _____

_____

4. Susan may go to Europe this summer _____

_____

Write compound sentences of your own, using the coordinating conjunctions
listed below. Remember to place a comma before the coordinating conjunction
that divides the clauses, and make certain that each of your clauses contains at
least one subject and one verb.

5. and: _____

_____

6. but: _____

_____

7. for: _____

_____

8. nor: _____

_____

9. or: _____

_____

10. so: _____

_____

11. yet: _____

_____

Construct four compound sentences punctuated with semicolons. In two of them, use a conjunctive adverb in the second clause.

12. _____

_____

13. _____

_____

14. _____

_____

15. _____

_____

Add commas and semicolons to the following sentences wherever they are needed. If a sentence needs no additional punctuation (in other words, if the sentence is simple rather than compound), label it *C* for *correct* in the left margin.

1. Have you noticed how many female singers have recently become very popular?

2. Back in the eighties, Madonna was probably the only female singer people might name but the nineties have spawned a whole host of female performers.

3. Certainly, there have always been wonderful female singers great performers from the French Edith Piaf to the soulful Aretha Franklin have entranced audiences for decades.

4. Most of these singers did not always sing their own songs they were the beautiful voices for other people's words.

5. During the sixties, several female singers did write their own music or they were part of groups that created original songs.

6. Do you remember Janis Joplin or Grace Slick of Jefferson Starship?

7. Today's female songbirds are similarly talented yet there is a subtle difference in their kind of music.

8. Alanis Morissette, Mariah Carey, and Sheryl Crow have all had remarkable hits in the mid-nineties and have attracted lots of fans.

9. Something seems to be happening to the way women project themselves their music suggests a new, more open, and spirited type of woman.

10. Alanis Morissette's songs readily come to mind for they are surprising in so many ways.

11. She appeared on a popular children's TV channel and seemed like just another child performer.

12. Her songs do not reflect an innocent child indeed they make explicit sexual references.

13. Along with her overt sexual references has come the impression of a very angry person and a very tough woman.

14. In her major hit "You Oughta Know" she yelled at her boyfriend for leaving her for another woman furthermore she devised several possible nasty revenge scenes in the song.

15. Everyone loved it the young girls, especially, bought it in droves and sang it as often as possible.

16. Some people doubt the sincerity of her anger however many listeners find this anger very appealing.

17. Through her music, she communicates that women do not have to see themselves as quiet and passive they can see themselves as strong and outspoken.

18. Popular music can tell us about ourselves in so many varied and fascinating ways!

Part One.   All the sentence patterns listed below have multiple subjects, multiple verbs, or both. But some patterns are for *simple* sentences, and other patterns are for *compound* sentences. Write a sentence for each pattern. If a sentence is *compound,* apply one of the two punctuation rules for compound sentences.

1. S-V-V: _____

_____

_____

2. S-V-S-V: _____

_____

_____

3. S-V-V-S-V: _____

_____

_____

4. S-S-V: _____

_____

_____

5. S-V-V-V: _____

_____

_____

6. S-V-S-S-V: _____

_____

_____

7. S-S-V-V: _____

_____

_____

Part Two. Combine each pair of simple sentences into one *compound* sentence. Try to use different conjunctions for each sentence, including some conjunctive adverbs.

8. We must sell our house in the next two months. We are already looking for a realtor.

_____

_____

9. Snow covered the field. The football game was played anyway.

_____

_____

10. I may get a job after graduation. I may attend graduate school.

_____

_____

11. Mr. Johnson is sixty-four years old. He could retire next year.

_____

_____

12. I want to lose weight. I don't like to diet.

_____

_____

13. All my term papers are completed. Now I can relax.

_____

_____

_____

10

Complex and Compound-Complex Sentences

Complex Sentences

There are two kinds of clauses, independent and dependent. As you have seen in Lesson 9, **independent clauses** can stand alone as complete sentences. For example,

I was ill.

We loved the play.

A **dependent clause,** however, *cannot* stand alone as a complete sentence. Instead, it must be attached to, or *depend* upon, an *independent* clause in order to form a grammatically complete sentence and to express a complete idea. Notice that the following dependent clauses are not complete sentences.

When he comes over . . .

If we come to the play . . .

Before we saw the movie . . .

Harcourt Brace & Company

These clauses seem incomplete because they are actually only part of a sentence. Using the first of the following sentences as a model, change each dependent clause into a complete sentence by adding an appropriate *independent* clause.

When he comes over, *we watch TV.*

If we come to the play, _____

_____

Before we saw the movie, _____

_____

You have now constructed two complex sentences. A **complex sentence** contains both independent and dependent clauses. (In contrast, a **compound sentence** contains only *independent* clauses.)

Every dependent clause begins with a subordinating conjunction. A **conjunction** joins words or groups of words. The conjunctions that begin dependent clauses are called **subordinating conjunctions** because the word *subordinate* means "of lesser importance." Grammatically speaking, a dependent clause is "less important" than an independent clause because it cannot stand alone as a complete sentence. In contrast, the conjunctions that you used in the previous lesson to form compound sentences are called **coordinating conjunctions** because *coordinate* means "of equal importance." Since both of the clauses in a compound sentence are independent, both clauses are "of equal importance."

The type of dependent clause that you will be studying in this lesson is called an adverb clause because, like other adverbs, an **adverb clause** describes a verb (or sometimes an adjective or an adverb). It is the same kind of clause that you worked with in Lesson 2. The subordinating conjunctions used to begin adverb clauses describe verbs by telling *how, when, where, why,* or *under what conditions* the action occurs.

how: as if, as though

when: after, as, as soon as, before, until, when, whenever, while

where: where, wherever

why: because, in order that, since, so that

under what conditions: although, as long as, even though, if, though, unless

Read the following sentences. A slanted line indicates the point at which each sentence divides into two separate clauses. Underline the subject of each clause *once* and the verb *twice*. Circle the subordinating conjunction.

While we studied / he watched TV.

I babysat / so that they could go to a movie.

As long as we communicate, / we will remain friends.

Now examine the clause in each sentence that contains the circled subordinating conjunction.

The clause that contains the subordinating conjunction is the dependent clause.

Notice that in a complex sentence, the dependent clause may be either the first or the second clause in the sentence.

When Julia sings, she is very happy.

Rick finds time to exercise *after he finishes work.*

In most cases, the adverb clauses in a complex sentence are *reversible.* That is, the sentence has the same basic meaning no matter which clause comes first. For example,

When he takes the train, he usually reads his books.

He usually reads his books *when he takes the train.*

or

If we go on vacation, we will have lots of fun.

We will have lots of fun *if we go on vacation.*

However, the order of the clauses in a complex sentence does affect the punctuation of the sentence.

1. If the **dependent** clause is the first clause in the sentence, it is followed by a comma.

Before she performed at the club, Stephanie welcomed her guests.

Harcourt Brace & Company

2. If the **independent** clause is the first clause in the sentence, no comma is needed.

Stephanie welcomed her guests *before she performed at the club.*

Punctuate the following complex sentences. First circle the subordinating conjunction in each sentence, and draw a slanted line between the clauses.

After we eat dinner we're going to see a movie.

The child carries her teddy bear with her wherever she goes.

If it doesn't rain the crops will be ruined.

As soon as I finish painting my apartment I'll help you paint yours.

Compound-Complex Sentences

When a compound sentence includes a dependent clause, that type of sentence is called a **compound-complex** sentence. The dependent clause may be in either main clause.

I rushed to the store, but I had forgotten my wallet *when I parked the car.*

or

Although I want to get a better job, I *don't want to leave this city,* and my family doesn't want to move either.

In compound-complex sentences we can see the operation of all the punctuation rules that we have studied up to now. In the examples below of compound-complex sentences, notice how important it is to recognize the three different types of joining words: coordinating conjunctions, subordinating conjunctions, and conjunctive adverbs. (See chart on inside front cover.)

The independent clauses of a compound-complex sentence may be joined with a comma and a coordinating conjunction.

The scientist presented his findings, but the audience was unimpressed *after* he finished his talk.

Harcourt Brace & Company

The independent clauses of a compound-complex sentence may be joined with only a semicolon.

Popular culture is sometimes confusing; the information is fascinating to study *even though* it is not always simple to interpret.

When a conjunctive adverb is used to join the independent clauses, a semi-colon is needed between the independent clauses.

A lot of new television shows have sexual content; *however,* there seems to be a trend back to family programming *although* it may take a long time for these shows to become popular.

When a dependent adverbial clause comes *after* an independent clause, it is *not* set off with a comma.

I rarely go to concerts, *but* I do love classical music *because* it sounds so very beautiful.

or

I do love classical music *because* it sounds so beautiful, *but* I rarely go to concerts.

When a dependent adverbial clause comes in front of an independent clause, it *is* set off with a comma.

I rarely go to concerts, *but because* it sounds so beautiful, I love classical music.

or

Because it sounds so beautiful, I love classical music, *but* I rarely go to concerts.

The following sentences are **complex.** First, underline the dependent clause in each sentence. Then add a comma to the sentence if it is necessary. If a sentence needs no additional punctuation, label it *C* for *correct.*

1. Because I am a college professor I spend much of my time indoors in class-rooms, libraries, and my office.

2. Therefore, I like to get outdoors whenever I have the time to relax.

3. My gardens are places where I spend a lot of my free time.

4. As soon as I get home from work I take a look at my front and back yards.

5. The front of my house is landscaped as though it were an English country garden.

6. The plants have been chosen so that some flowers are in bloom all year long.

7. A year-round garden is possible since I live in the mild climate of Southern California.

8. The lavender and verbena and pansies make me feel as if I were in the English countryside instead of in the middle of Los Angeles.

9. A peaceful yard is important to me because I live only a block from one of Los Angeles' busiest freeways.

10. As long as I can enjoy my gardens I can ignore the thousands of cars pass-ing near my house.

The remainder of this exercise includes both complex and compound-complex sentences. First, underline the dependent clause in each sentence. Then add a comma and/or a semicolon if necessary. If a sentence needs no additional punctu-ation, label it *C* for *correct.*

11. The backyard is a place where my husband often spends his free time.

12. Although part of our backyard is devoted to roses most of it is a vegetable garden.

13. We have a large vegetable garden because one of our children is a vegetarian so she eats a lot of fresh vegetables and fruit.

14. We always raise tomatoes since home-grown tomatoes taste so much better than the ones in the market.

15. After you eat a home-grown tomato you will never be satisfied with the commercial varieties and you will want to start a garden of your own.

16. Some of our vegetables may seem unfamiliar if you do not eat Asian food.

17. We grow Japanese eggplants, Chinese string beans, and Korean edible chrysanthemums so that we have the ingredients for our favorite Asian dishes close at hand.

18. Perhaps you are wondering if Japanese eggplants and Chinese string beans are significantly different from their American counterparts.

19. While American eggplants are large and football-shaped Japanese eggplants are small and narrow and about the size of zucchini.

20. Although Chinese string beans taste like American string beans they are as thin as pencils and they grow to two feet or more in length.

21. Since we also eat American food we grow lettuce, squash, green peppers, strawberries, and melons.

22. We would like to grow even more plants but we can't unless we can find more space.

Harcourt Brace & Company

The essay below includes simple, compound, complex, and compound-complex sentences, but they are not always punctuated correctly. Correct all punctuation errors.

Most of us have grown up with Walt Disney animations. From Mickey Mouse and Donald Duck to the longer tales of *Bambi,* and *Cinderella,* Disney cartoons have played an important role in our childhoods. Generally, we think about childhood as an innocent and carefree period because it is not burdened with the weight of adult concerns and Disney has been part of that innocent time. However, things seem to be changing with Disney and maybe these changes reflect changes in our society.

One change in Disney animations is their depiction of female characters. Have you noticed how different the recent Disney female heroines are from those in Disney's early works? When *Snow White* was created women understood their social role in a very clear way for they saw their role as that of homemaker and mother. Think about Snow White's behavior when she first finds the Seven Dwarfs' house. Because it is very dirty she puts on an apron and starts to clean

Harcourt Brace & Company

moreover she winds up treating the dwarfs as if they were her children. She is innocent, maternal, and somewhat childlike.

Disney's recent heroines are very different and they very much reflect our new ideas about women and their roles. Belle in *Beauty and the Beast* is very strong, intelligent, and not interested in the man who wants to marry her. She is very much a new, independent young woman. Ariel in *The Little Mermaid* is also independent. Disney changed the original story to make Ariel a rebellious teenager although this was a change that angered and distressed some people.

Even more recently, Meg in *Hercules,* Esmeralda in *The Hunchback of Notre Dame,* Jasmine in *Aladdin,* and Pocahontas reflect Disney's attempt to portray characters of different ethnic origins. Pocahontas is very powerful and independent but not as powerful as Esmeralda. A gypsy, Esmeralda is clearly the ethnic heroine of the story for she is strong, clever, and the center of all the action.

Another change is that many of the recent characters also very sensual and this is a new attribute for Disney females. Although many of the earlier Disney women wore revealing clothing and had hourglass figures now their sensuality has become a plot device and is intentional. Compare, for example, Meg and Snow White. Meg intentionally tries to attract Hercules, while Snow White does nothing to try to attract

Harcourt Brace & Company

Prince Charming. They both get their man but they use very different means.

The transition from Snow White and Cinderella to Esmeralda and Meg marks extraordinary changes in the way Disney now projects the image of women. Certainly these animations suggest a great deal about our culture's views of women and about how far women have come since Snow White wore an apron and swept the seven dwarf's cottage as she chastised them for their lack of cleanliness!

Harcourt Brace & Company

Part One. Combine each pair of sentences into a single complex sentence by joining them with a subordinating conjunction. Think carefully: Which sentence will make the best dependent clause and which conjunction will make a meaningful connection? Use as many different conjunctions as possible. Punctuate your new complex sentence.

1. Julia won the presidential medal. She is a fine athlete.

_____

_____

2. Benjy played soccer well. We cheered.

_____

_____

3. We clapped. Allen finished his performance.

_____

_____

4. I will go to Hawaii this summer. I can save enough money.

_____

_____

Part Two. In this section, there are several groups of simple sentences. Combine each group into a single compound-complex sentence by using the various ways for connecting clauses that you've studied in the past lessons. Make sure your new sentence makes sense and reads smoothly. (Several combinations are possible. You might want to try writing each sentence on a piece of scratch paper first.) The first sentence combination has been done as an example.

Harcourt Brace & Company

5. The store was having a sale.

The merchandise didn't appeal to me.

I didn't buy anything.

Although the store was having a sale, the merchandise didn't appeal to me, so I didn't buy anything.

6. Dean loves his music.

His neighbors hate it.

He plays it loudly.

_____

_____

_____

7. The winter is here.

The storms are ferocious.

We built a fire.

_____

_____

_____

8. Jules wanted a kitten.

He promised to care for it.

His mother takes care of it now.

_____

_____

_____

Harcourt Brace & Company

9. The team lost the game.

The players were discouraged.

The coach gave them a pep-talk.

_____

_____

_____

_____

10. The job paid well.

The hours were inconvenient.

Bob decided to work somewhere else.

_____

_____

_____

_____

11. We are planning a party for our boss.

He is retiring next month.

I am responsible for buying the gift.

_____

_____

_____

_____

_____

12. Tofu is good for you.

It provides lots of protein.

We don't like the way it tastes.

_____

_____

_____

Harcourt Brace & Company

Avoiding Run-On Sentences and Comma Splices

As you learned in Lesson 9, a compound sentence consists of at least two independent clauses. The independent clauses in a compound sentence must be separated either by a coordinating conjunction (such as *and, but, or*) preceded by a comma or by a semicolon if no conjunction is used.

Failure to separate two independent clauses results in an error known as a **run-on sentence.** The following are examples of run-on sentences.

I don't play tennis well I have a poor backhand.

The next game is at our school we want to go to it.

Run-on sentences are very serious errors. They are not only confusing to the reader, but they also indicate that the writer cannot tell where one sentence ends and another begins.

There are three ways to correct a run-on sentence.

1. Divide the run-on into two separate sentences, ending each sentence with a period. (If the sentences are questions, end them with question marks.)

    I don't play tennis well. I have a poor backhand.
    The next game is at our school. We want to go to it.

Although this method produces grammatically correct sentences, an essay written completely in short simple sentences creates the choppy effect of an elementary school reading text. Therefore, you should also consider using the two other methods of correcting run-ons.

2. Change the run-on to a **compound sentence** by separating the clauses with a semicolon or with a coordinating conjunction preceded by a comma.

    I don't play tennis well; I have a poor backhand.

                              or

    I don't play tennis well, *for* I have a poor backhand.
    The next game is at our school; we want to go to it.

                              or

    The next game is at our school, *so* we want to go to it.

As you learned previously, the relationship between the two clauses in a compound sentence is often clearer if a conjunction is used rather than a semicolon.

3. Change the run-on to a complex sentence by placing a subordinating conjunction before one of the clauses.

    Because I have a poor backhand, I don't play tennis well.
    Because the next game is at our school, we want to go to it.

Another very common error is the comma splice. Unlike a run-on, in which two independent clauses are run together with no punctuation, a **comma splice** consists of two independent clauses joined with *not enough* punctuation—that is, with only a comma (and *no* coordinating conjunction). The following are examples of comma splices.

122

I didn't finish the novel, it was boring.

Bob needs a new car, he can't afford to buy one now.

A comma by itself is *not* a strong enough punctuation mark to separate two independent clauses. Only periods and semicolons can be used without conjunctions to separate independent clauses. Comma splices can be corrected by the same three methods used for correcting run-on sentences.

1. Divide the comma splice into two separate sentences.

I didn't finish the novel. It was boring.

Bob needs a new car. He can't afford to buy one now.

2. Change the comma splice into a **compound sentence** by separating the clauses with either a coordinating conjunction *and* a comma or with a semicolon.

I didn't finish the novel, *for* it was boring.

or

I didn't finish the novel; it was boring.

Bob needs a new car, *but* he can't afford to buy one now

or

Bob needs a new car; he can't afford to buy one now.

3. Change the comma splice into a **complex sentence** by placing a subordinating conjunction before one of the clauses.

I didn't finish the novel *because* it was boring.

Although Bob needs a new car, he can't afford to buy one now.

Remember that if the dependent clause (the clause continuing the subordinating conjunction) is the first clause in the sentence, it should be followed by a comma.

Correct the following run-on sentences and comma splices:

I would like to visit Hawaii I have many relatives there.
All my sisters have blue eyes I do not.
Gary is used to cold weather, he grew up in Minnesota.
They are always in debt they have too many credit cards.
Sue has many problems, she always manages to look cheerful.

Harcourt Brace & Company

Correct all the run-on sentences and comma splices. If a sentence is neither a run-on nor a comma splice, label it *C* for *correct* in the left margin.

1. The United States is a nation of immigrants, each group of immigrants has brought its own food to this country.

2. Americans frequently eat food from other countries some of these foods are now thought of as being typically American.

3. Hot dogs and hamburgers are good examples, few Americans now consider these foods to be German.

4. However, hot dogs were originally known as "frankfurters" this German city was famous for a sausage made in long, reddish links.

5. Another name for hot dogs is "wieners" this is a short form of the German *Wienerwurst,* meaning "Vienna sausage."

6. The residents of Hamburg, Germany, had a recipe for ground beef called "Hamburg steak" it was Americans who put hamburger patties into buns.

7. People in Germany still eat sausages and ground beef other American ethnic foods are unknown in their supposed countries of origin.

8. No one in China eats chop suey this is strictly an American dish.

9. At first, chop suey was prepared and eaten only by Chinese immigrant laborers it quickly became popular with American miners and railroad workers.

10. Americans think of tacos as being typically Mexican American-style tacos are not a traditional Mexican dish.

11. Pizza is also an Americanized food American pizza is very different from the Italian version.

12. Italian pizzas lack the fancy toppings common in the United States, a traditional pizza in southern Italy is topped with only chopped garlic and olive oil.

13. Pasta is also served differently in Italy than in the United States in Italy it is usually served before the main course rather than being a main dish.

14. A recent addition to American menus is pita bread it was brought to the United States by immigrants from the Middle East.

15. The two halves of a piece of pita form a pocket this makes pita bread a convenient container for a sandwich filling.

16. Greek and Persian fast-food restaurants sell pita sandwiches filled with roast lamb or fried chickpeas, these are now a popular lunch item.

17. Americans have adopted foods from other countries American food is also eaten in foreign countries throughout the world.

18. Of course, much of that so-called "American" food consists of hot dogs, hamburgers, and pizza!

Each of the paragraphs below contains comma splices and run-on sentences. Correct these errors using the methods you have learned from this and previous lessons.

August of 1996 was special in the history of our civilization, many interesting events happen all the time, but that month NASA revealed something astonishing.

NASA scientists shared a phenomenal discovery, life may have existed on Mars. The scientists presented their intriguing data and a stunning piece of evidence at a news conference this evidence showed the press and the world a rock containing a microscopic Martian life form. The scientists went on to explain how life might have begun on a planet other than ours. They talked about the rock extensively and showed a short film explaining their new findings.

Many people have wondered if we truly are alone in the universe certainly lots of science fiction stories and movies reflect this fascination, *War of the Worlds* by H.G. Wells captured the imagination of people early in this century, curiously, in the summer of 1996, one of the most popular movies was *Independence Day,* this movie, like *War of the Worlds,* was about Earth being threatened by invading

Harcourt Brace & Company

aliens the rock from Mars has nothing to do with a Martian invasion, however, science fiction suddenly looks a little more plausible.

This new discovery is very exciting. This new life form may be from Mars it is certainly not from Earth. Is there life on other planets only time will tell.

Part One. Show that you understand what a **run-on sentence** is by writing three of them in the spaces provided below. After you write each run-on, correct it. Try to use different methods in correcting your run-ons.

1. _____

_____

correction: _____

_____

2. _____

_____

correction: _____

_____

3. _____

_____

correction: _____

_____

Show that you understand what a **comma splice** is by writing three of them in the spaces provided below. After you write each comma splice, correct it. Try to use different methods to correct your comma splices.

4. _____

_____

correction: _____

Harcourt Brace & Company

5. _____

_____

correction: _____

_____

6. _____

_____

correction: _____

_____

_____

Part Two. Write *two different* corrections for each of the following run-on sentences.

7. Our team should have won the game we ended up losing.

correction: _____

_____

correction: _____

_____

_____

8. Mr. Swenson went to two different doctors he got two different diagnoses.

correction: _____

_____

correction: _____

_____

_____

Write *two different* corrections for each of the following comma splices.

9. The company refused to raise salaries, the employees decided to strike.

correction: _____

_____

correction: _____

_____

10. She wants to get a job, she can't find anyone to care for her children.

correction: _____

_____

correction: _____

_____

Correcting
Fragments

The basic unit of expression in written English is the sentence. As you already know, *a sentence must contain at least one independent clause.*

If you take a group of words that is *not* a complete sentence and punctuate it as though it were a complete sentence, you have created a **sentence fragment.** In other words, you have written only a piece—a fragment—of a sentence rather than a complete sentence.

As you can see. These groups of words. Are fragments.

Since semicolons and periods are usually interchangeable, fragments may also be created by misusing semicolons. If you look carefully at the following two groups of words, you will see that they should form a single complex sentence which needs only a comma, and not a semicolon.

As you can see; wrong punctuation may be confusing.

As you can see, wrong punctuation may be confusing.

Although fragments occur frequently in speech and occasionally in informal writing, they are generally not acceptable in classroom writing and should be avoided in formal writing situations.

There are two types of fragments: **dependent clauses** and **phrases.**

As you have already learned (Lesson 10), a dependent clause cannot stand alone as a complete sentence. It must be attached to an independent clause in order to form a complex sentence.

Therefore, any dependent clause that is separated from its main clause by a period or semicolon is a fragment.

Below are several examples of this type of fragment.

When we arrived at the theater. The movie had already begun.

When we arrived at the theater; the movie had already begun.

We'll miss our plane. If we don't hurry.

We'll miss our plane; if we don't hurry.

Eliminate the dependent clause fragments in the following paragraph by punctuating them correctly.

Because we are trying to eat more healthful food. We are buying more fruits and vegetables. The problem occurs. Whenever we go to a restaurant. At the restaurant, we find that desire takes over; although we have the best of intentions to eat only healthful foods. If we were at home; we would never think of eating pies and ice cream. Since the menu is so intriguing. We wind up ordering things no one would consider to be healthy. When we order banana splits and ice cream; it isn't healthy, but we sure are happy.

Are you remembering to punctuate each dependent clause according to its location? As you learned in Lesson 10, if the *dependent* clause is the first clause in a sentence, it should be followed by a comma. If the *independent* clause is the first clause in a sentence, no comma is needed.

The second type of fragment is the **phrase.** Since a phrase is defined as a group of words that does not contain both a subject and a verb, a phrase obviously cannot be a complete sentence. *All phrases are fragments.* Study the following types of fragments, and notice the way each phrase has been changed from a fragment into a complete sentence.

FRAGMENT—NO SUBJECT	Had seen that film.
SENTENCE	*We* had seen that film.
FRAGMENT—NO VERB	The children on the bus.
SENTENCE	The children rode on the bus.
FRAGMENT—INCOMPLETE VERB (-ING FORM)	Kevin attending a conference.
SENTENCE	Kevin *was attending* a conference.

(An -ing main verb must be preceded by a helping verb.)

or

Kevin *attended* a conference.

(Change the -ing verb to a main verb.)

FRAGMENT—INCOMPLETE VERB (PAST PARTICIPLE)	The garden filled with flowers.
SENTENCE	The garden *is filled* with flowers.

(To be a main verb, a past participle must be preceded by a helping verb. See Lesson 25 for an explanation and a list of past participles.)

FRAGMENT—INFINITIVE	To do well in school.
SENTENCE	*Students must study* hard to do well in school.
FRAGMENT—PARTICIPIAL PHRASE	Being a good friend.
SENTENCE	Being a good friend *takes* a lot of hard work.

The following groups of words are fragments because they lack either a subject or a verb or because they have an incomplete verb. Rewrite each fragment so that it becomes a complete sentence.

The weather being much too cold for swimming.

Ate a pizza for lunch yesterday.

Praying for a good turnout.

The candidate knowing that his lead would not hold.

A present sent by air mail.

The house damaged by the tornado.

The city's new subway system.

When you are writing a composition, be careful not to separate a phrase from the rest of the sentence to which it belongs.

INCORRECT	I'm looking for a small puppy. With floppy white ears.
CORRECT	I'm looking for a small puppy with floppy white ears.
INCORRECT	Wanting to do well; he studied all night.
CORRECT	Wanting to do well, he studied all night.

Rewrite the following items so that any fragments are correctly joined with the sentences to which they belong.

I burned my hand. While frying chicken for dinner.

Pleased with the pianist's performance. The audience demanded an encore.

Susan lay sleeping on the beach. From noon until three o'clock.

To summarize: **phrases** are sentence fragments because they do not contain both a subject and a complete verb. (In other words, they are not clauses.) **Dependent clauses** are fragments because they are not *independent* clauses. This is simply another way of stating the most basic rule of sentence construction:

Every sentence must contain at least one independent clause.

Harcourt Brace & Company

Correct all of the fragments in the following essay. Some corrections will require attaching phrases or dependent clauses to the independent clauses to which they belong. Other corrections will require adding subjects and verbs or changing participles to main verbs. In some cases, a comma should be substituted for a semicolon.

Attending powwows is a favorite summer activity for my family. A powwow being a ceremonial gathering of American Indians. There are many powwows in my area. Since Southern California has a large Native American population.

Although some powwows take place in indoor arenas. They are usually held outdoors. Spectators gather around a large circular area. To be used for dances. The powwow begins with a parade. Called the Grand Entry. At the beginning of the parade is an honor guard. Carrying the American and American Indian flags. Following them are military veterans. They are the modern equivalent of the Native American warriors of the past.

Following the veterans are dancers. Wearing colorful costumes. The costumes vary according to the type of dance their wearers will perform. For example, male "Traditional" dancers wear the kind of clothing. That most people think of as being typically Indian. Their costumes including deerskin leggings, beaded vests, and feather bonnets. They also wear a bustle consisting of a semicircle of feathers. Tied to their lower backs. Female Traditional dancers wear beautifully decorated dresses. And carry fringed shawls and eagle feather fans. Other types of dancers including Fancy dancers, Grass dancers, and Jingle dancers. Each type of dancer having a distinctive costume.

Dance contests are major events in a powwow. The judges watch. As each group of dancers performs. The dancers wear numbers. So that the judges can identify them easily. The dancers ranging in age from toddlers to the elderly. The music provided by groups of singers who accompany their songs by beating a large drum.

There are also giveaway ceremonies. Where a family honors one of its members. By distributing gifts to friends, relatives, and honored guests.

While waiting for the next event to start; people can visit booths where artisans display and sell Native American wares. They can also buy snacks. Like fry bread and Indian tacos.

It is an inspiring event. To see people preserving the traditions of their ancestors. And passing them on to their children.

The paragraphs below contains *comma splices, run-ons,* and *fragments.* Correct these errors using the methods you have learned from this and previous lessons.

Several years ago, a movie called *Close Encounters of the Third Kind* caught the imagination of the public, it was about people. Having experiences with life from another planet, another film called *E.T.* also dealt with this possibility, do you think we have been visited by extraterrestrial beings?

Many people believe in this possibility. And in the possibility of "unidentified flying objects." Or, UFOs. In the nineties, several television shows explored UFOs as their subject matter, these include a show called *Sightings.* And one called *The X Files.* Movies also dealt with this subject too, like *Independence Day.*

This interest in extraterrestial life has a very long history. Going all the way back to 1947 and a place called Roswell, New Mexico. No one actually knows what happened at that time there is a story that has continued to be told for about fifty years now. The story describing a flying saucer with alien life forms on it crashing in the Roswell desert.

The story contains some extraordinary claims. Because it says that the United States government found this space ship and its life forms. Three of the life forms supposedly dead and one still alive. Although it later died also. According to the story, the whole report is still kept secret in a place called Area 51. Apparently a special hiding place about which only a few people in the government know anything.

This story presumes that special agencies in the government keeping this information from us this would mean that extraterrestrial life truly exists. These ideas are exciting. And also a little scary. No one really knows for sure. What is true. Some people think this story is simply nonsense, some people believe it is definitely true.

Do you believe? That we are not alone in the universe?

Harcourt Brace & Company

Show that you understand what **fragments** are by writing the kind of fragment described. After you write each fragment, correct it in the space provided.

1. a fragment with no subject

_____

_____

correction: _____

_____

_____

2. a fragment with no verb

_____

_____

correction: _____

_____

_____

3. a fragment with an incomplete verb

_____

_____

correction: _____

_____

4. a fragment with a past participle instead of a complete verb

_____

_____

correction: _____

_____

5. a dependent clause separated from a main clause by a semicolon

_____

_____

correction: _____

_____

6. a dependent clause separated from a main clause by a period

_____

_____

correction: _____

_____

Identifying and Punctuating the Main Types of Sentences

Correct any run-on sentences, comma splices, or fragments in the following paragraphs.

Although Americans are rarely thought of as great fans of poetry. We have a quiet love affair with our poets. Most of us were introduced to poetry in school sometimes, we even had to memorize poems.

Because television, films, and computers seem to absorb so much of our attention. Many people believe that poetry might just die out, the opposite appears to be happening. Poetry readings happening everywhere. Everyone wanting to be a poet. Of some sort.

Lots of bookstores and coffeehouses offer poetry readings nightly these nights are a lot of fun. Because anybody can stand up and read a poem. Men, women, old, and young try their hand at this ancient art. Sometimes the poetry is exciting or beautiful terrible poetry is also read. Since anyone can say he or she is a poet.

The good part of all of these readings is that poetry lives. It lives in coffeehouse readings. In books, as well as in song lyrics. A lot of the finest and most interesting poetry today coming from music. Ranging from Bob Dylan's anti-war songs of the early 1970s to the Beatles and even to Kurt Cobain!

Harcourt Brace & Company

Identifying and Punctuating the Main Types of Sentences

Correct any errors you find in the following paragraphs. These paragraphs reflect the rules covered in Unit Three.

1. Growing up today can be difficult, every teenager has experienced the strains of this period. The situation was a bit different in the past. When young people were teenagers during the early part of this century; there was less time for leisure. Lots of adolescents needed to work in order to help out their families economic times were difficult, many families lived on farms where each family member needed to pull his or her own weight. During the first half of this century; people tended to get married early. By the time a person was twenty, he or she might be married and have a child or two there was little time to play and explore life.

2. Today, teenagers take a much longer time to grow up in fact sometimes, an individual can remain in adolescence into his or her thirties! Many young adults in their twenties still live at home with their parents, others return home after being divorced. Women now may put off having babies until their thirties, or even their forties and there are stories about men in their seventies fathering children.

Harcourt Brace & Company

Although Peter Pan was a character from the Victorian era; there seem to be a whole lot of people who would like to be Peter Pan today "I don't want to grow up" could be the motto of more than one generation.

3. Growing up for some teenagers does not mean attending college. Fighting a powerfully difficult environment. These young people struggle to find a way into adulthood, some young people must deal with streets; filled with crime. Drugs may haunt their lives. Because many young people have little money and drug dealing can provide huge amounts of income. Some teenagers become drug dealers or become part of gangs that sell drugs. A young person may be confronted with violence and even death. While just going for a walk in the neighborhood. For a lot of teenagers; growing up in the city poses many problems. Probably the worst of these problems being the problem of gangs and crime.

Parenthetical Expressions

When speaking, people often interrupt their sentences with expressions such as *by the way, after all,* or *as a matter of fact.* These expressions are not really part of the main idea of the sentence; instead, they are interrupting—or **parenthetical**— expressions. In speech, people indicate that these parenthetical expressions are not part of the main idea of the sentence by pausing and dropping their voices before and after the expression. In writing, the same pauses are indicated with commas.

You have already learned that commas may be used to separate the clauses in compound and complex sentences. Another major function of the comma is to "set off" interrupting or **parenthetical expressions** from the rest of the sentence in which they occur.

Read the following sentences aloud, and notice how the commas around the italicized parenthetical expressions correspond to the pauses you make in speech.

Well, I guess I have to leave now.

She's only a child, *after all.*

Did you know, *by the way,* that we're getting a new boss?

The rule for punctuating parenthetical expressions is very simple:

A parenthetical expression must be completely set off from the rest of the sentence by commas.

This means that if the parenthetical expression occurs at the *beginning* of the sentence, it is *followed* by a comma. For example,

No, I don't know where they keep their knives.

If the parenthetical expression is at the *end* of the sentence, it is *preceded* by a comma.

He will be late again, *I suppose.*

If the parenthetical expression is in the *middle* of the sentence, it is both *preceded* and *followed* by a comma.

Her sister, *on the other hand,* is very popular.

There are many parenthetical expressions. Some of the most frequently used ones are listed below:

after all

as a matter of fact

at any rate

etc. (an abbreviation of the Latin words *et cetera,* meaning "and other things")

for example

for instance

furthermore

however

in fact

nevertheless

Harcourt Brace & Company

of course

on the other hand

on the whole

therefore

well (at the beginning of a sentence)

yes and *no* (at the beginning of a sentence)

Expressions such as the following are often parenthetical if they occur in a position *other than* at the beginning of a sentence:

does it

doesn't it

I believe

I suppose

I hope

I think

is it

isn't it

that is

you know

For example,

He won the election, I believe.

Smoking, you know, is bad for your health.

Continual repetition of the parenthetical expression *you know* should be avoided in both speech and writing. If you are speaking clearly and your listener is paying attention, he knows what you are saying and does not have to be constantly reminded of the fact. Besides, you know, continually repeating *you know* can be irritating to your listener, and, you know, it doesn't really accomplish anything.

Study the following points carefully.

1. Some of the above words and phrases can be either parenthetical or not parenthetical, depending upon how they are used in a sentence.

If an expression is parenthetical, it can be removed from the sentence, and what remains will still be a complete sentence.

PARENTHETICAL	The problems, *after all,* are difficult.
NOT PARENTHETICAL	He failed *even after* all his efforts.
PARENTHETICAL	There is a football game today, *I believe.*
NOT PARENTHETICAL	*I believe* what you tell me.

2. Since the abbreviation *etc.* is parenthetical, it must be *preceded* and *followed* by a comma if it occurs in the middle of a sentence.

Books, stationary, art supplies, *etc.,* are sold at the corner store.

The final comma after *etc.* indicates that *etc.* is parenthetical. Notice that this comma serves a different function from the commas that separate the items in the series.

3. Conjunctive adverbs, like *however* and *nevertheless,* are considered parenthetical and are set off from the clause in which they occur. They should be punctuated in simple sentences as follows:

I thought the plan was a secret. *However,* everyone seems to know about it.

or

I thought the plan was a secret. Everyone, *however,* seems to know about it.

In the second clause of a compound sentence, **conjunctive adverbs** should be punctuated as follows:

Harcourt Brace & Company

She earns a good salary; *nevertheless,* she always seems to be borrowing money from her friends.

The concert was long; *however,* it was quite beautiful.

The semicolon is needed because the clauses in the compound sentence are not joined by a coordinating conjunction. The semicolon also takes the place of the comma that would normally precede a parenthetical expression occurring in the middle of a sentence. A comma follows the parenthetical expression to set it off from the remainder of the sentence. (Conjunctive adverbs have been discussed earlier in Lesson 9. For a complete list of them see the inside front cover of this book.)

4. People's names and titles are also set off by commas *if you are speaking directly to them* in a sentence. This type of construction is called **direct address.** The punctuation of direct address is the same as that used for parenthetical expressions.

Have you played your guitar today, *Allen?*

Ladies and gentlemen, please be seated.

Notice that names and titles are set off by commas only when the person is being *directly addressed* in the sentence. Otherwise, no commas are needed.

Music has always been important to Allen. (no commas)

Allen, have you always loved music? (commas for direct address)

Harcourt Brace & Company

Add commas and semicolons to the following sentences wherever they are needed. If a sentence needs no additional punctuation, label it *C* for *correct*. This exercise deals only with the punctuation of parenthetical expressions.

1. The O.J. Simpson trials captured the public's imagination didn't they?

2. After all how many times has one man been tried twice in so short a period?

3. The trials however were more than legal proceedings; they were also extra-ordinary media events.

4. Network television stations broadcast extensive portions of the first trial moreover some cable channels provided gavel-to-gavel coverage of the entire proceedings.

5. Articles about the trial appeared in newspapers, news magazines, tabloids etc. throughout the course of the trial.

6. As a matter of fact there were Internet sites that discussed the case.

7. The judge in the second trial banned radio and television coverage inside the courtroom however this did not deter one enterprising television station.

8. This station hired actors to dramatize the trial by of course using a transcript of the previous day's court proceedings.

9. After each of the trials, many of the principals in the case were interviewed on television in addition some of them wrote books about the trial.

10. Books were written for example by prosecution and defense attorneys, members of the jury, and relatives of the victims.

11. In fact several of the police officers involved in the case also authored books.

12. The best known of these police authors was of course Mark Fuhrmann.

Harcourt Brace & Company

13. O.J. Simpson himself I believe published a book and a videotape.

14. After all this media coverage, some people no longer wanted to hear about the trials.

15. On the other hand a Los Angeles television station broadcast a psychologist giving advice to Simpson trial "addicts" who might suffer withdrawal symptoms after the trials were over!

Add commas and semicolons to the following sentences wherever they are necessary. This exercise covers the punctuation of parenthetical expressions.

Well few of us consider things out of the ordinary except maybe when we are forced to. Sometimes events just make us pay attention to things we never even thought about as a matter of fact they can make us change our whole outlook on life. When these things happen, it can often be a dizzying experience.

Several events have happened during the last half of the twentieth century that have made a lot of changes in how we look at life in fact for some people, life has never been the same. World War II for example made us aware of some very disturbing things in human nature. Almost everyone is aware of the Holocaust in Europe as a matter of fact, we are still trying very hard to understand how this event occurred in such a seemingly civilized world. What for example does this event say about human nature? After all we have always thought that advances in technology went along with advances in moral behavior. But after World War II, we have come to recognize that a society can be very advanced and still be capable of doing terrible things.

Harcourt Brace & Company

Therefore I believe that World War II marked a change in how we as a culture came to regard human beings. Furthermore other events also shocked us during the latter part of the twentieth century. For instance the United States saw three political figures assassinated within a very short time span. Of course you know I mean John F. Kennedy, Robert Kennedy, and Martin Luther King, Jr.

At any rate historical events always have some great impact on us, and sometimes, the impact is good. Did you know that it was in the 1960s that man first walked on the moon? We have made tremendous strides to control a lot of illnesses so that people can live longer. In addition probably the one thing that will impact us the most, is the computer and the role cybernetics will play in our lives.

Well these are only a few of the events and changes that may have influenced us. We are all in this great adventure together and of course we will keep you aware of what comes next!

Add commas and semicolons to the following essay wherever they are necessary. This exercise covers the punctuation of parenthetical expressions. (Note: This essay contains slang and other examples of informal usage.)

You know I have tried really hard to let my parents in on the music and things I love, but somehow, things just haven't worked out too well.

On the one hand my dad wants to be with me, but on the other hand when he hangs with me, he gets really annoyed. For example my friends and I love to go dancing. Now dance music for my dad isn't ballroom dancing after all he grew up in the sixties and loved the Beatles. However my music is something else!

For instance I really love Hip Hop and both West Coast and East Coast Rap. Whenever I listen to this music, my parents have a verifiable fit. It isn't that I blast the music or even push it in their faces, but as soon as they hear the sound of rap, they simply blow fuses.

So of course my dad wants to go dancing with us. Well I should have known this was one big mistake however I must have been hoping for a miracle. To my dad, dancing means something quite different than it does to us. He has never heard of Techno or Trance or House or Jungle music for example. So when he came with us to some clubs, he was asking for some surprises.

Yes it was one big mistake. Dad had no idea how loud the music was going to be, or how repetitive it was. Dance music is very electronic, and it has a very hypnotic quality that can be very annoying and boring if you're not into it. Dad of course wasn't into it at all furthermore he thought the whole club scene was too crowded, too weird, and too loud.

I guess I should have known that taking Dad out to a club with a bunch of the guys wasn't going to work but on the other hand I was touched I suppose by his effort to show interest in my life.

Next time Dad wants to do something, it makes more sense to go to a movie or a baseball game I think. After all there are a lot of things for us to do that won't make him feel like he was born in prehistoric times!

Appositives

In sentences you sometimes use a noun whose meaning may not be as clear to your reader as it is to you. For example, suppose that you write:

Mr. Anderson needs to sign these forms.

If you think that your reader may not know who Mr. Anderson is, you can add a phrase to your sentence to provide more information about him.

Mr. Anderson, *the Director of the Financial Aid Department,* needs to sign these forms.

This kind of explanatory phrase is called an **appositive** (from the verb to *appose,* meaning "to place things beside each other"). An appositive is a phrase placed beside a noun in order to clarify that noun's meaning. Study the following sentences, in which the appositives have been italicized. Notice that each appositive *immediately follows the noun it describes.*

July, *the seventh month in our calendar,* was named after Julius Caesar.

The center of the farm workers' movement was Delano, *a small town north of Bakersfield, California.*

Poi, *the staple food of the Hawaiian diet,* is made from taro root.

As you can see, appositives must be set off by commas from the rest of the sentence just as parenthetical expressions are. Appositives are considered *extra* elements in a sentence because they add additional information about a noun that has already been *specifically identified.* For example, in the sentence about *July* above, even without the appositive "the seventh month in our calendar," you know which month was named after Julius Caesar because the month has been specifically identified as *July.* In the next example, even without the appositive "a small town north of Bakersfield, California," you know that the town which was the center of the farm workers' movement is *Delano.* In the third example, even without the appositive "the staple food of the Hawaiian diet," the food is specifically identified as *poi.*

Here is the rule for punctuating this kind of explanatory phrase or clause:

If a phrase or clause adds additional information about a noun that has already been specifically identified, that phrase or clause must be completely set off from the rest of the sentence by commas.

In this lesson, you will be dealing with appositives, which are phrases. In Lesson 15, you will be applying the same rule to clauses.

Specifically identified includes mentioning either a person's first or last name, or both, or using words such as "my oldest brother," "my ten o'clock class on Monday," or "my hometown." The nouns in the last three phrases are considered to be *specifically identified* because even though you have not mentioned your brother's name, you can have only one "oldest" brother. Similarly, only one specific class can be your "ten o'clock class on Monday," and only one specific town can be your "hometown." In other words, *specifically identified* means limiting the meaning of a general word like *town* to *one particular town* or limiting a general word like *class* to *one particular class.*

Underline the appositives in the following sentences, and then punctuate them. Remember that appositives *follow* the nouns that they describe.

My oldest brother a doctor at Queen of Angels Hospital is attending a medical convention in San Francisco.

My twelve o'clock class on Tuesday English 110 concentrates on writing.

This summer I'm going to visit my hometown Salinas, California.

Boston, Massachusetts the home of many universities is my favorite city to visit.

Each spring I return to San Francisco the city of hills and cable cars.

On the other hand, if a phrase is *necessary* to establish the specific identity of a noun, it is *not set off* by commas. Study the difference between the following pair of sentences.

The novel *Great Expectations* is considered by many critics to be Charles Dickens's greatest work. (No commas are used to set off *Great Expectations* because the title is necessary to identify which of Dickens' many novels is considered to be his greatest work.)

Charles Dickens' fourteenth novel, *Great Expectations,* is considered by many critics to be his greatest work. (Commas are used to set off *Great Expectations* because Dickens' greatest work has already been specifically identified as his *fourteenth* novel.)

Most single-word appositives are necessary to establish the specific identity of the nouns they follow and are, therefore, *not* set off by commas.

The color *yellow* is my favorite.

My sister *Susan* lives in Detroit.

The word *penurious* means "stingy."

Underline the appositives in the following sentences, and then add commas wherever they are necessary. Some sentences may not require commas.

Fiat automobiles are manufactured in Turin a city in northeastern Italy.

The komodor a Hungarian sheepdog has a coat that looks like a mop.

Balboa a sixteenth-century Spanish explorer was the first European to discover the American side of the Pacific Ocean.

Harcourt Brace & Company

In Europe, fruits and vegetables are usually sold by the kilogram an amount equal to 2.2 pounds.

My older brother an orthopedic surgeon spends much of his time working on injured athletes.

Have you seen the movie *Titanic*?

Add commas to the following sentences wherever they are necessary. If a sentence needs no additional punctuation, label it *C* for *correct*. This exercise covers only the punctuation of appositives.

1. Every October, a news bulletin from Stockholm, Sweden, announces the winner of the Nobel Prize for literature the world's highest honor for writers.

2. The Nobel Prize is named for Alfred Nobel the Swedish inventor of dynamite.

3. When Alfred Nobel died in 1896, he left his entire fortune an estate of nearly nine million dollars to be used for five annual awards.

4. Three of the awards are for discoveries in chemistry, physics, and medicine three areas of science of particular interest to Nobel.

5. Another award is the Peace Prize an honor won by people like Martin Luther King, Jr., and Mother Teresa.

6. The final award the Nobel Prize for Literature honors an author's entire body of work rather than just a single book.

7. In 1993, the Nobel Prize for Literature was awarded to Toni Morrison an American writer.

8. Morrison is best known for her novels stories dealing with the African American experience.

9. Other American Nobel Prize writers include the 1962 winner John Steinbeck the author of the novel *The Grapes of Wrath*.

10. *The Grapes of Wrath* the story of migrant farmers from Oklahoma is one of the most famous novels written during the American Depression.

11. William Faulkner one of the greatest American writers of the twentieth century won the Nobel Prize in 1949.

12. Faulkner was a resident of Mississippi the setting for many of his works, including *The Sound and the Fury* his most famous novel.

13. Most students have read some fiction by Ernest Hemingway the winner of the 1954 prize.

14. His novel *The Old Man and the Sea* is often read in American literature courses.

15. Less famous today than the previously mentioned American authors is the 1938 winner Pearl Buck the first woman ever to receive the literature prize.

16. Buck's novel *The Good Earth* a moving story of a Chinese peasant family is her best-known work.

17. Buck the daughter of American missionaries grew up in China and wrote many books about that country.

18. As of 1996, American authors had won eight Nobel Prizes a national total exceeded only by France's thirteen award winners.

Add commas and semicolons to the following sentences wherever they are necessary. If a sentence needs no additional punctuation, label it *C* for *correct*. This exercise covers punctuation rules from Lessons 13 and 14.

1. Most English-speaking people are not familiar with Norse mythology the stories of the gods and heroes of ancient Scandinavia.

2. However the names of some Norse gods are an important part of our English vocabulary.

3. In fact four of our days of the week are named after Norse gods.

4. Wednesday for example is named after Woden the sky father.

5. Woden held a position similar to that of the Greek god Zeus.

6. Thursday is named after Thor the Norse god of thunder.

7. Tuesday once known as Tiu's Day is named after Tiu the god of war.

8. Friday is named after a goddess in fact there are two possible sources for this day's name.

9. One is the goddess Frigg the wife of Woden.

10. However some scholars believe that Friday is named after Freya the goddess of love and beauty.

11. Another Norse goddess did not lend her name to a day of the week nevertheless her name is also a part of our modern vocabulary.

12. She is Hel the goddess of the dead.

13. You can of course guess which English word carries her name.

14. How did the people of England become familiar with the gods of Scandinavia a region far to the north of England?

15. During the fifth century A.D., England was invaded by the Angles, the Saxons, and the Jutes three tribes from Denmark and northern Germany.

16. These tribes conquered the Celtic inhabitants of Britain, and consequently their mythology became a part of English culture.

17. As a matter of fact one of the earliest and most famous epic poems in English literature is *Beowulf* the story of a Scandinavian hero.

Part One. The sentences below are arranged in pairs. Combine each pair into a third sentence. Use information from the second sentence *to create an appositive in the first sentence.* Decide whether or not you should set off the appositive with commas. The first pair has been done as an example.

1. a. John Gray's first book became a runaway best-seller.

 b. His bestseller was *Men Are from Mars, Women Are from Venus.*

 c. *John Gray's first book,* Men Are from Mars, Women Are from Venus, *became a runaway best-seller.*

2. a. California has a huge immigrant population.

 b. California is the Sunshine State.

 c. _____

3. a. Detroit was once America's center for car making.

 b. Detroit is called the Motor City.

 c. _____

4. a. Disney made a movie about Hercules.

 b. Hercules was an ancient Greek hero.

 c. _____

5. a. My uncle just arrived from Spain.

 b. My uncle's name is Juan Carlos.

 c. _____

6. a. Argentina has a very European lifestyle.

b. Argentina is a country with many Italian and German immigrants.

c. _____

Part Two. Add appositives to the following sentences. If necessary, set off the appositives with commas. The first sentence has been done as an example.

7. I visit my old college, *Syracuse,* each spring.

8. The television program _____ is very controversial.

9. The TV personality _____ may make some movies.

10. My favorite novel _____ is on our English reading list.

11. The heavy metal band _____ just made a new CD.

12. McDonald's _____ opened even in Moscow.

13. Bill Clinton _____ was elected for a second term.

14. Aiesha _____ just bought a new car.

15. *Star Wars* _____ continues to be very popular.

Restrictive and Nonrestrictive Clauses

In Lesson 14 you learned that if a phrase adds extra information about a noun that has already been specifically identified, that phrase (an **appositive**) must be set off by commas. For example,

> Many of NBC's television shows are filmed in Burbank, *a city in the San Fernando Valley.*

The appositive is set off by commas because the place in which many of NBC's television shows are filmed has already been specifically identified as *Burbank.*

On the other hand, if a phrase is necessary to establish the specific identity of a noun, the phrase is *not* set off by commas.

> The verb *to be* is the most irregular verb in the English language.

The phrase *to be* is not set off by commas because it is necessary to identify which specific verb is the most irregular verb in the English language.

Harcourt Brace & Company

The same rule that applies to the punctuation of appositive phrases also applies to the punctuation of *clauses.* Read the following sentences, in which the dependent clauses have been italicized. Can you see why one sentence in each pair has commas while the other does not?

The woman *whom you have just met* is in charge of the program.

Teresa Gomez, *whom you have just met,* is in charge of the program.

The book *which I am now reading* is an anthology of African American literature.

Black Voices, which I am now reading, is an anthology of African American literature.

In the first sentence of each pair, the dependent clause is necessary to establish the specific identity of the noun it follows. This type of clause is called a **restrictive** clause because it *restricts,* or limits, the meaning of the word it describes. For example, in the first sentence if the restrictive clause were removed, the sentence would read:

The woman is in charge of the program.

The meaning of this sentence is unclear since there are billions of women in the world, and any one of them might be in charge of the program. But when the clause is added to the sentence, the meaning of the general word "woman" is now restricted, or limited, to *one particular woman—the woman whom you have just met.* Thus, the restrictive clause "whom you have just met" establishes the specific identity of the word "woman."

Similarly, in the third sentence above, the clause "which I am now reading" identifies *which* book is in an anthology of African-American literature. It restricts the general word "book" to *one particular book—the book which I am now reading.*

Since restrictive clauses are necessary to establish the specific identity of the nouns they describe, the following punctuation rule applies:

Restrictive clauses are not set off by commas.

In contrast, the clauses in the second and fourth sentences are *not* necessary to identify which particular woman is in charge of the program or which particular book is an anthology of African American literature. In these sentences, the woman has already been identified as *Teresa Gomez,* and the book has already been identified as *Black Voices.* Since these clauses are *not* restrictive clauses, they are called **nonrestrictive clauses.** Nonrestrictive clauses merely add extra information about the nouns they describe. They serve the same function as appositives and are punctuated in the same way.

Nonrestrictive clauses must be completely set off from by the rest of the sentence commas.

This means that if a nonrestrictive clause is at the *end* of a sentence, it will be *preceded* by a comma. If it is in the *middle* of a sentence, it will be *both preceded and followed* by a comma. (Like appositives, nonrestrictive clauses never occur at the beginning of a sentence since they must follow the noun that they describe.)

The restrictive and nonrestrictive clauses that you have been studying are called **adjective clauses** because, like adjectives, these clauses describe nouns. The words that most frequently introduce adjective clauses are:

that

where

which

who

whom

whose

Like all clauses, adjective clauses must contain both a subject and a verb. But notice that in adjective clauses *the word that introduces the clause may also be the subject of the clause.*

S   V

The house *which once occupied this lot* was destroyed by fire.

Or the clause may contain a separate subject:

S V

The wallet *that I lost* contained all my credit cards.

Harcourt Brace & Company

Adjective clauses, like adverb clauses, are used in **complex sentences.** Although these sentences may not seem to be complex at first glance, if you study the sentences above, you will see that each of them has two subjects and two verbs. Also, if the adjective clause, which is the **dependent clause,** is removed from the sentence, a complete independent clause remains.

INDEPENDENT CLAUSE

S   V

The house was destroyed by fire.

DEPENDENT CLAUSE

S   V

which once occupied this lot

INDEPENDENT CLAUSE

S   V

The wallet contained all my credit cards.

DEPENDENT CLAUSE

S V

that I lost

An adjective clause often occurs in the middle of a sentence since it must follow the noun it describes. When an adjective clause is in the middle of a sentence, part of the independent clause precedes it, and the rest of the independent clause follows it. For example,

S V

Food *which is high in calories* often tastes better than low-calorie food.

S   S   V

The Joy Luck Club, which originally was a novel, has also been made into a movie.

A sentence may contain more than one adjective clause. Each clause is punctuated separately. In the following sentences, the first adjective clause is *non-restrictive* (with commas), and the second clause is *restrictive* (no commas).

The San Fernando Valley, *which suffered a large earthquake in 1994,* has since experienced aftershocks *that distress many people.*

The Cadillac automobile, *which was originally manufactured in Detroit,* is named after the French explorer *who founded the city.*

172

Underline every adjective clause in each of the following sentences, and circle the noun that it describes. Then decide which clauses are restrictive (and do *not* need commas) and which clauses are nonrestrictive (and *do* need commas). Add the appropriate punctuation.

Note: Although clauses beginning with *who, whom, whose, where,* or *which* may be either restrictive or nonrestrictive, clauses which begin with *that* are *always* restrictive.

Union Square which is one of San Francisco's main shopping areas is known for its open-air flower stalls.

The classes that I am taking this semester are all easy for me.

Most tourists who come to Los Angeles also visit Disneyland which is less than an hour's drive from the city.

The candidate whom we supported was not elected.

Ms. Gomez whose native language is Spanish also speaks French, German, and English.

He is an artist whom we all admire a great deal.

Each of the following sentences contains one or more adjective clauses. Underline each adjective clause, and circle the noun or pronouns it describes. If the clause is nonrestrictive and needs additional punctuation, add a comma or commas wherever they are necessary. If all of the adjective clauses in a sentence are restrictive and the sentence needs no additional punctuation, label it C for *correct*.

1. Thu Ha who is in my English class has traveled a long way to come to college.

2. It is not just the distance from her adoptive parents' home which is at least 500 miles away.

3. She has traveled a long way psychologically from her original family's home which is in Vietnam.

4. The community that Thu grew up in was a farm community.

5. It was a community where few children had the chance to get a good education.

6. Thu's family which was very close was killed in the Vietnam War.

7. Thu was adopted by an American family who heard of her plight.

8. The American lifestyle which is fast-paced was confusing to her.

9. The many cars, the neon lights, and the noise were very different from her family's farm which was quiet and peaceful.

10. Her new parents who were very understanding people tried to help her adjust.

11. Thu who can be shy didn't make many friends at school.

12. A girl who was from Mexico started to talk to her in class one day.

13. Angelina who was also new to the United States was just as bewildered as Thu.

14. Angelina came from a medium-sized town that was just outside of Chihuahua.

15. Although she had been attending school, she was not accustomed to American life which is much more hectic.

16. Thu and Angelina helped each other with their English lessons which were very hard for both of them.

17. They also became good friends who went everywhere together.

18. They helped each other adjust to the American lifestyle which soon became less bewildering.

19. Now both of them are going to a community college which is in their town.

Add commas and semicolons to the essay below wherever they are necessary. This exercise covers the punctuation rules in Lessons 13–15.

People who want to know more about eighteenth-century American life can visit Williamsburg the capital of colonial Virginia. Williamsburg has been carefully restored to its eighteenth-century appearance in fact it is often called a "museum city." Within the mile-long historical area of Williamsburg are more than a hundred buildings and furthermore over a hundred gardens. Eighty-eight buildings are original; the others have been reconstructured.

What makes Williamsburg unusual however is that it is a *living* museum. Many of the shops are occupied by real people who pretend to be eighteenth-century Williamsburg inhabitants. They wear costumes that are like those of colonial times, and they speak in the English dialect that was used in Virginia during the eighteenth century. For example a printer may explain to visitors how his eighteenth-century printing press works, or tourists can watch a blacksmith whose tools are identical to those used by smiths two hundred years ago.

Harcourt Brace & Company

Besides the shops, other interesting places to visit are the town's taverns. They include Wetherburn's Tavern where George Washington was a frequent visitor and Raleigh Tavern where Colonel Patrick Henry had dinner with his fellow army officers. Today, we tend to think of taverns as places only for drinking however in colonial times they also served meals, hosted dances, and were places to gamble and play billiards. Taverns were therefore important gathering places. In fact many of the political discussions leading to the American Revolution may have occurred in Williamsburg's taverns since the men who visited them were among this country's founding fathers. They include for example Thomas Jefferson the author of the Declaration of Independence and the third president of the United States and George Wyler America's first law professor as well as the first Virginian to sign the Declaration of Independence.

Another popular site especially for children is the town *gaol* the British spelling of jail. Visitors can see the small cells which once housed Blackbeard's pirates, and children can lock each other up in the pillory and stocks two common forms of punishment during colonial times.

After a day of sightseeing, tourists can dine at a restaurant that serves typical eighteenth-century meals and can also attend a candle-lit con-

Harcourt Brace & Company

cert in the Governor's Palace a beautiful colonial mansion. Then they can retire to one of the many hotels and inns that surround the town to sleep in rooms that contain reproductions of colonial American furniture.

Harcourt Brace & Company

Part One. Construct your own complex sentences using the words listed below to form *restrictive* clauses. Underline the adjective clause in each of your sentences, and circle the noun it describes.

1. whose: _____

_____

2. who: _____

_____

3. that: _____

_____

4. which: _____

_____

Part Two. Construct your own complex sentences using the words listed below to form *nonrestrictive* clauses. Underline the adjective clause in each of your sentences, and circle the noun it describes. Use appropriate punctuation.

5. who: _____

_____

6. whom: _____

_____

7. which: _____

_____

8. whose: _____

_____

Part Three. Underline the adjective clauses in the following sentences, and circle the word which each clause describes. If the clause is nonrestrictive, add the necessary punctuation. If the clause is restrictive, the sentence needs no additional punctuation, so label it *C* for *correct*.

9. Los Angeles has many famous streets which capture our imagination.

10. Some of the people who live here never actually visit these famous places.

11. A street that lots of people like to go to is Melrose Avenue.

12. Melrose which is a street favored by young people runs several miles from West Hollywood almost to downtown.

13. The stores that attract so much attention on Melrose are very diverse.

14. Anyone can find just about any item that he or she desires.

15. There are many clothing stores, trendy stores, crazy poster stores, jewelry stores, shoe stores, and restaurants that boggle the mind.

16. Aardvarks which sells vintage clothing attracts people from all over the world.

17. If you want pasta and pizza that is out of this world or great Chinese food which makes Chinatown pale or 1950s hamburger joints which make you dream of Elvis and rock and roll, then this is the place!

18. One of my favorite stores is Maya which sells jewelry and odd, exotic items.

19. There is also a great store that sells wind-up toys which will take you back to your childhood.

20. Melrose Avenue is certainly one of the best places that Los Angeles has to offer.

Items in a Series and Dates and Addresses

A **series** consists of *three or more* related items. Commas are placed between each item in a series in order to separate the items from each other. The final comma before the conjunction is optional.

> *Danish, Swedish,* and *Norwegian* are related languages.

> or

> *Danish, Swedish* and *Norwegian* are related languages.

If *every* item in a series is joined by a conjunction (*and, or,* or *nor*), no commas are needed since the conjunctions keep the individual items separated. This type of construction is used only when the writer wishes to place particular emphasis on the number of items in the series.

> *Soup* and *salad* and *dessert* are included in the price of your meal.

If a date or an address consists of more than one item, a comma is used after *each* part of the date or the address, *including a comma after the last item.* (If the last item in the series is also the last word in the sentence, only a period follows it.) Notice that this punctuation rule differs from the rule used for punctuating an ordinary series.

My grandparents will celebrate their fiftieth wedding anniversary on October 11, 1999, with a party for all of their family.

The name of the month and the number of the day (October 11) are considered a single item and are separated from the year by a comma. However, notice that a comma also *follows* 1999, which is the last item in the date.

We moved from Norman, Oklahoma, to Flagstaff, Arizona, in 1995.

Notice the commas after "Oklahoma" and "Arizona." These commas are used in addition to the commas that separate the names of the cities from the names of the states.

If a date or an address consists of only a single item, no comma is necessary.

December 25 is Christmas.
We moved from Oklahoma to Arizona.

A comma is not used before a zip code number.

The mailing address for Hollywood is Los Angeles, California 90028.

Punctuate the following sentences.

The armistice signed on November 11 1918 ended the fighting in World War One.

Because of the multi-ethnic character of my neighborhood, church bazaars sell tacos pizza teriyaki chow mein and hot dogs.

The coffee shop's special club sandwich contains ham and cheese and turkey.

I can't believe that you drove from Portland Oregon to Newark New Jersey in three days.

John F. Kennedy Aldous Huxley and C.S. Lewis all died on November 22 1963.

Add commas to the following sentences wherever they are needed. If a sentence needs no additional commas, label it *C* for *correct.* This exercise covers only the punctuation rules from Lesson 16.

1. Louisa May Alcott (1832–1888) wrote many novels for young girls, including *Little Women Little Men* and *Jo's Boys.*

2. Her family's home at 399 Lexington Road Concord Massachusetts has been preserved as a museum and is open to the public.

3. When you visit Plymouth Massachusetts be sure to see the historical sites of Plymouth Rock Plimoth Plantation and the *Mayflower II.*

4. Paul Revere's famous midnight ride took place of April 18 1775 near Lexington Massachusetts.

5. Los Angeles City College is located near Hollywood at 855 North Vermont Avenue Los Angeles California 90029.

6. You have from October 1 1998 till March 31 1999 to enter this contest.

7. Is it possible to drive from Las Vegas Nevada to Santa Fe New Mexico in a single day?

8. The last major battle of the American Revolutionary War ended on October 19 1781 at Yorktown Virginia.

9. Korean meals include soup rice and vegetables in addition to the main course.

10. October 29 1929 was the date of the worst stock market crash in American history.

11. I can't believe you plan to take chemistry and physics and biology in the same semester.

12. Before you get a driver's license, you must take a written exam have an eye test and pass a driving test.

Add semicolons and commas wherever they are necessary in the following essay. This exercise covers all the lessons on punctuation in Unit Four.

The members of the Beltran family are planning to spend their summer vacation in our nation's capital Washington D.C. They will leave their home in Portland Oregon and fly to Washington on Monday July 12th. Their family includes the parents Tony and Alma and their three children Jimmy Tina and Oscar.

Rather than staying in Washington, the Beltrans have chosen the Holiday Inn 8777 Georgia Avenue in nearby Silver Springs Maryland. This hotel has a swimming pool an exercise room and its own restaurant moreover children who are under the age of twelve get free meals. The free meals for the younger two Beltran children will of course save the family a considerable amount of money.

Furthermore the hotel is only two blocks from the Silver Springs Metro Station where the Beltrans can take a subway to Washington D.C. The Beltrans think that using the subway and other public transportation will be cheaper than renting a car in fact they have been warned not to drive in Washington because of the city's traffic

Harcourt Brace & Company

problems. For example Washington has many one-way streets. During the morning, the traffic on these streets flows into the capital however at four in the afternoon the direction of the traffic suddenly changes so that drivers can use the same streets to leave the city. Being on these one-way streets at four o'clock can of course be an unsettling experience for drivers who find themselves suddenly heading in the wrong direction or for those whose watches do not show the correct time.

Back in Portland, the Beltrans have spent a long time choosing the places they want to visit in Washington. They wanted to select places that the whole family will enjoy. Of course there are some places that every tourist must see therefore the Beltrans will be sure to visit the White House the Lincoln Memorial and the Washington Monument. In addition Oscar who loves animals wants to see the National Zoo which has a giant panda a gift from the People's Republic of China. Tina who hopes to be an artist someday wants to see the National Gallery of Art, and Jimmy a lover of airplanes casts his vote for the National Air and Space Museum. Alma on the other hand wants to visit the Folger Shakespeare Library because she is a high school English teacher. Finally, Tony a Vietnam War veteran plans to visit the Vietnam Veterans' Memorial.

Harcourt Brace & Company

Add commas and semicolons to the following paragraphs wherever they are necessary. Do not add periods to make separate sentences. This exercise covers all the rules in Unit Four.

Lots of people have heard about Orange and Los Angeles counties in Southern California however few people know about San Bernardino County the largest county in the United States.

San Bernardino County which is east of Los Angeles has many exciting and interesting attractions. For example there is the University of Redlands. The University of Redlands a small liberal arts school has a wonderful experimental college called Johnston College which was begun in the early seventies. The classes at Johnston are innovative and provocative, and students are not graded in a traditional fashion.

Almost everybody has heard about Palm Springs, but few know that it is part of San Bernardino County. Palm Springs the playground of movie stars has beautiful hotels great restaurants and wonderful recreational centers. You can swim golf play tennis hike etc. when you visit Palm Springs. Because most people think of Palm Springs as a desert, few realize how close it is to mountains with snow.

If you are like most Americans, you may have never realized how varied a region Southern California is. With deserts snowcapped mountains and seaside resorts, it is a wonderful place. Hidden in this paradise is San Bernardino County a region as varied and wonderful as the rest of Southern California. No wonder it is called the Inland Empire!

Add commas and semicolons to the following sentences wherever they're necessary. Do not add periods to make separate sentences.

Just about everybody seems interested in relationships in fact magazines are filled with articles about how to get a man keep a man know a man likes you etc. Then of course there are all those self-help books which address just about every issue about relationships that anyone of us could ever imagine!

The authors mostly psychologists or would-be psychologists have addressed diverse subjects. For example Deborah Tannen a linguistics professor at Georgetown University writes about linguistic differences in the talk between men and women. Her books *You Just Don't Understand, Talking from Nine to Five,* and *That's Not What I Meant!* have had a significant influence from universities to bedrooms.

Although both men and women are interested in relationships, mainly women it seems buy these books. If on the other hand a man has a book, he probably got it from a woman. Even the titles of the books suggest that the audience is made up of women. For example recent books include *Men Who Can't Love, What Smart Women Know Ten Stupid Things Women Do* and of course *Men are from Mars, Women are from Venus.* The author of the last book John Gray has made a fortune from this and other books, as well as from a series of videos.

You know it seems we all must be pretty confused about things. I mean so many books try to tell us how to do the things that should come naturally however I simply can't figure it all out. At any rate we will probably continue to buy these books as we stumble down that road toward happiness!

Punctuation that "Sets Off" or Separates

Correct any punctuation mistakes you find in the following paragraphs. Besides adding commas and semicolons, you may also have to *remove* incorrect punctuation marks.

The Museum of African American History opened on April 12 1997 at 315 East Warren Avenue in Detroit Michigan. This museum which cost 39 million dollars was paid for primarily with taxpayer dollars, however private individuals and businesses also made contributions. The businesses, which contributed to the museum, include KMart local banks and of course the automobile manufacturers for which Detroit is famous.

The museum's 120,000-square-foot building has a permanent exhibit and, in addition two galleries for changing exhibits. The permanent exhibit which is the largest exhibition ever created about African Americans depicts important eras in the African American experience, including slavery the Reconstruction the Harlem Renaissance and the civil rights struggle. It includes a replica of one of the ships, that was used to transport slaves from West Africa to the New World. Furthermore the ship's hull lists the names of all the other ships that carried slaves to this country. An unusual part of this exhibit is the sculptures of fifty young slaves aboard the ship. Their faces are castings made from teenagers, who live in the Detroit area. Among other items from more recent times is a dress worn by Carlotta Wells one of the nine children who integrated Central High School in Little Rock Arkansas and the flight suit worn by Mae Jemison an astronaut on the space shuttle Endeavor. There is even a reproduction of the door to the jail cell in Birmingham Alabama where Dr. Martin Luther King, Jr., was imprisoned. Besides being a place to view historical artifacts, the museum also hopes to be an educational center therefore it also contains classrooms and a research library.

It is appropriate that this museum is located in Detroit which has a population that is 80 percent African American. However museum officials also hope to attract visitors from outside the Detroit area, in fact they want the museum to become one of the city's main cultural and tourist attractions. Perhaps you the readers of this essay will be among the museum's future visitors.

PRONOUN USAGE

17

Subject, Object, and Possessive Pronouns

Pronouns are words that are used to refer to persons, places, things, and ideas without repeating their names. In other words, pronouns are used in place of nouns. For example, rather than saying "Ben lost Ben's notebook last night, but Ben found the notebook this morning," you can say, "Ben lost *his* notebook last night, but *he* found *it* this morning." In this sentence, the pronoun *his* replaces *Ben*'s, the pronoun *he* replaces *Ben,* and the pronoun *it* replaces *notebook.* The noun that the pronoun replaces is called the **antecedent** (Latin for "to go before") of the pronoun.

There are several different kinds of pronouns, but in this lesson you will be studying only **subject pronouns, object pronouns,** and **possessive pronouns.**

Singular Pronouns		
Subject	*Object*	*Possessive*
I	me	my, mine
you	you	your, yours,
he	him	his
she	her	her, hers
it	it	its

Plural Pronouns

Subject	Object	Possessive
we	us	our, ours
you	you	your, yours
they	them	their, theirs

As their name suggests, **subject pronouns** are used as the *subject* of a sentence or a clause. For example,

He is a good dancer.
We went to the park together.

In *formal* speech and writing, subject pronouns are also used after forms of the verb *be,* as in:

That is *she* singing with the chorus.
It is *I.*
If I were *she,* I'd have come to the lecture.

In formal speech and writing, subject pronouns are used after forms of the verb *be* because they refer to the *same* thing or person as the subject.

That = *she* singing with the chorus.
It = *I.*
I = *she*

However, in *informal* speech, many people would use object pronouns in the sentences below.

That is (or *That's*) *her* singing with the chorus.
It is (or *It's*) *me.*
If I were *her,* I'd have come to the lecture.

Whether you choose to say "it is I" or "it is me" depends upon the circumstances. If you are taking an English test or writing a formal essay, using subject pronouns after forms of *be* is appropriate and expected. But if you are speaking casually with a friend, "It is I" may sound artificial, and the informal "It is me" might be more suitable.

In this unit, you will be studying both grammar and usage. Try to keep clear in your mind those situations in which you have a choice between formal and informal constructions (usage) and those situations in which only one pronoun form is correct at all times (grammar).

"It is *we*" versus "It is *us*" = usage.

"Al and *I* are here" versus "Al and *me* are here" = grammar.

Object pronouns are used as objects of prepositions, as direct objects, and as indirect objects.

You will remember that the noun or pronoun in a prepositional phrase is called the **object of the preposition.** That is why an object pronoun replaces the noun. For example,

The award was given to *Matthew.*

The award was given to *him.*

Please sit by *Cathy.*

Please sit by *her.*

Object pronouns are also used as direct objects. A **direct object** is the word that *receives* the action of the verb and, with very few exceptions, follows the verb, often as the next word.

```
       S           DO
```
The artist painted that *picture.*

The artist painted *it.*

```
 S            DO
```
He composed that *song* last night.

He composed *it* last night.

Another way in which object pronouns are used is as indirect objects. An **indirect object** is the person or thing *to whom* or *for whom* something is done.

```
 S      IO         DO
```
She made *Robert* a chocolate cake.

She made *him* a chocolate cake.

The previous sentence is another way of saying, "She made a chocolate cake *for him.*"

```
   S           IO  DO
```
Benjamin gave his sister a gift.

Benjamin gave *her* a gift.

The previous sentence is another way of saying, "Benjamin gave a gift *to her.*"

Possessive pronouns are used to show ownership.

The cat scratched *its* neck.
The children stamped *their* feet in joy.

Very few people make pronoun errors when there is only one subject or one object in a sentence. For example, no native speaker of English would say, "Us is here" instead of "We are here." However, people often do make mistakes when two subjects or two objects are paired up in a sentence. For example, which of the following two sentences is grammatically correct?

Barbara bought Kevin and *me* some good cookies.
Barbara bought Kevin and *I* some good cookies.

To determine the correct pronoun in this kind of "double" construction, split the sentence in two like this:

1. Barbara bought Kevin some good cookies.
2. Barbara bought (me, I) some good cookies.

As you can tell after you have split the sentence in two, it would be incorrect to say "Barbara bought *I* some good cookies." The correct pronoun is *me,* which is the indirect object of the verb *gave.* Therefore the whole sentence should read:

Barbara bought Kevin and *me* some good cookies.

Which of the following two sentences is correct?

The mayor congratulated Rick and *I.*
The mayor congratulated Rick and *me.*

Again, split the sentences in two.

1. The mayor congratulated Rick.
2. The mayor congratulated (me, I).

198

Now, which pronoun is correct?

Another very common pronoun error is using subject pronouns instead of object pronouns after prepositions. The object of a preposition must be an *object* pronoun. Which of the following two sentences is correct?

The teacher handed new books to Sam and *I.*
The teacher handed new books to Sam and *me.*

If you split the sentence in two, you have:

1. The teacher handed new books to Sam.
2. The teacher handed new books to (me, I).

The correct pronoun is *me,* which is the object of the preposition *to.* Therefore, the correct sentence is:

The teacher handed new books to Sam and *me.*

It is extremely important that you do not decide which pronoun to use simply on the basis of what "sounds better" *unless you split the sentence in two first.* To many people, "The teacher handed new books to Sam and *I*" sounds more "correct" than "The teacher handed new books to Sam and *me,*" yet, as you have seen, *me* is actually the correct pronoun.

Another example of choosing an incorrect pronoun because it "sounds better" is the frequent misuse of the subject pronoun *I* after the preposition *between.* As you already know, the object of a preposition must be an *object* pronoun. Therefore, it is always incorrect to say "between you and *I.*" The correct construction is "between you and *me.*"

Circle the pronoun that correctly completes each of the following sentences.

Between you and (I, me), that's a wonderful movie.
The teacher rewarded Joseph and (I, me) for our presentation.
Ken and (she, her) speak frequently.
Helene made Sasha and (I, me) Halloween costumes.
The party was for their class and (we, us).

Occasionally you may use constructions like the following:

We freshmen must pre-enroll for our classes.
Most of *us nurses* would prefer to work the 7 A.M. to 3 P.M. shift.

Harcourt Brace & Company

To determine whether the sentence requires a subject or an object pronoun, see which pronoun would be correct if the pronoun appeared in the sentence by itself rather than being followed by a noun.

(We, us) citizens should vote in each election.
(We, us) must vote in each election.
Give a raise to (we, us) good workers.
Give a raise to (we, us).

The correct pronouns are *we* citizens and *us* workers.

Circle the pronoun that correctly completes each of the following sentences.

Some theaters give a discount to (we, us) students.
Actors depend on the support of (we, us) fans.
(We, us) customers want the store to stay open later.

The first part of this exercise is intended for a quick review of subject and object pronouns. Reverse each sentence so that the subject pronoun becomes the object and the object pronoun becomes the subject.

Example: *I* saw *them* at the play.
Answer: *They* saw *me* at the play.

1. *He* looked lovingly at *her.*

2. *They* gave *her* the gift.

3. *We* saw *them* today.

4. *I* wished *him* good health.

5. *She* asked *us* a question.

6. *You* told *him* the truth.

7. *We* baked *her* a birthday cake.

8. *I* sang *them* a song.

Circle the pronoun that correctly completes each sentence. Remember to split the sentence if it contains a "double" construction. Apply the rules of formal English usage.

9. My mother and (I, me) love movies.

10. He gave (her, she) a gift.

11. Between you and (I, me) that's a good idea.

12. (We, Us) students liked the test.

13. The actors performed for (we, us).

14. The teacher sat near him and (I, me).

15. The star players were (she, her) and Jan.

16. It is (me, I).

17. He spoke glowingly about Bill and (she, her).

18. The judges awarded John and (I, me) first place.

19. You can speak freely around Jim and (we, us).

20. He handed the tickets to Phillip and (I, me).

Some of the following sentences contain pronoun errors. Cross out the incorrect pronouns, and write in the correct forms. If a sentence contains no pronoun errors, label it *C* for *correct*. Apply the rules of formal English usage.

1. Several people sat between Ben and I.

2. Us women like some independence.

3. Your gift was a big surprise to my husband and I.

4. After talking about those girls and I, the teachers looked pleased.

5. Ice skating usually causes Bob and me to want lots of hot chocolate!

6. Hal and him wrote the play in about six months.

7. Allen and she walk the dog every night at eight o'clock.

8. It was us who came over late last night.

9. In the event that you don't get this letter, you and him should probably still come to the game.

10. Surprisingly, it was I who won the lottery.

11. Between you and I, this pasta is just great!

12. The dense fog made Bob and I very nervous.

13. Neither Bob nor me felt that we ought to be driving.

14. Because us both are so cautious, we pulled over to the side of the road.

15. Unfortunately, the car's battery died, causing both him and me to get a little anxious.

16. Who could rescue him and me?

17. A car filled with laughing children saved we poor souls, and they even handed us some pizza slices.

18. However, that cheese pizza gave both of us terrible stomach pains.

19. Him and me wound up at the hospital, but at least we weren't lost in the fog!

Harcourt Brace & Company

Part One. Give the following sentences two subjects by adding a subject pronoun to each sentence. *Use a different pronoun for each sentence.* Apply the rules of formal English usage. The first sentence has been done as an example.

and they
1. The boys ^ played ball well.

2. The students went to the lecture.

3. My friend went to a movie.

4. My cousin sang in the church choir.

5. The children handed out flowers.

6. Barry ran around the field.

7. Teresa played the flute in the orchestra.

Part Two. Give the following sentences two objects by adding an object pronoun to each sentence. *Use a different object pronoun for each sentence.* Apply the rules of formal English usage. The first sentence has been done as an example.

and her
8. Please give Bob ^ the lunch tickets.

9. The judge told the other jury members about the procedures.

10. He sat near Bill last night.

11. Roberto sang songs to Julia.

12. Benjamin played catch with Matthew.

13. Allen gave his phone and computer to Diane.

14. They looked for Maria at the dance.

15. Have you seen Sarah recently?

Harcourt Brace & Company

Pronouns in Comparisons and Pronouns with *-self, -selves*

Using Pronouns in Comparisons

In speech and in writing, we often compare two people or two things with each other. For example,

Rose is older than *I* am.

The company pays *Ellen* a higher salary than it pays *me.*

In the sentences above, it is easy to tell whether a subject pronoun or an object pronoun should be used in each comparison. In the first sentence, the subject pronoun *I* is correct because it would be clearly ungrammatical to say "Rose is older than *me* am." In the second sentence, the object pronoun *me* is correct because you would not say that "The company pays Ellen a higher salary than it pays *I.*"

However, people usually do not write out their comparisons completely. They use a shortened form instead. For example,

Harcourt Brace & Company

Mary Anne plays tennis better than *I.*
The accident injured Sam more than *me.*

In these cases, it is possible to determine which pronoun is correct by mentally filling in the words that have been left out of the comparison.

Mary Anne plays tennis better than I (do).
The accident injured Sam more than (it injured) me.

Fill in the missing words to determine which pronouns are correct in the following sentences.

Clarence can run longer distances than (I, me).
I enjoy classical music more than (he, him).
This trip will be more interesting for you than (she, her).
That dress looks better on you than (she, her).
Doing sit-ups is easier for you than (I, me).

When you fill in the missing words, the correct comparisons are

Clarence can run longer distances than *I* (can).
I enjoy classical music more than *he* (does).
This trip will be more interesting for you than (it will be for) *her.*
That dress looks better on you than (it does on) *her.*
Doing sit-ups is easier for you than (it is for) *me.*

In *informal* usage, you often hear people use object pronouns instead of subject pronouns in comparisons (for example, "He's taller than me" instead of "He's taller than I"). However, these forms are generally considered inappropriate in writing and formal speech. You should be especially careful in situations where the wrong pronoun can change the meaning of the entire sentence. For example, "Mary danced with George more than *I* (danced with him)" does not mean the same thing as "Mary danced with George more than (she danced with) *me.*" In addition, using the wrong pronoun can sometimes lead to unintentionally ridiculous sentences, like the following:

My husband likes sports more than me.

Unless the husband happens to like sports more than he likes his wife, the correct pronoun would be:

My husband likes sports more than (*I*) do.

(Note: The conjunction *than,* which is used in comparisons, should not be confused with the adverb *then.*)

Avoiding Doubled Subjects

Do not "double," or repeat, the subject of a sentence by repeating the noun in its pronoun form.

INCORRECT   My sister, she is a nurse.
CORRECT   My sister is a nurse.
INCORRECT   The Johnsons, they are our neighbors.
CORRECT   The Johnsons are our neighbors.

Pronouns with -self, -selves

Some pronouns end in *-self* or *-selves:*

Singular	**Plural**
myself	ourselves
yourself	yourselves
himself	themselves
herself	
itself	

These pronouns can be used in two ways. They can be **reflexive pronouns.** Reflexive pronouns are used when the object of the verb or the object of the preposition is the same person or thing as the subject. For example,

I cut *myself.* (myself = I)
They will do the job by *themselves.* (They = themselves)

The family enjoyed *themselves* at the party. (themselves = family)

Or they may be used for *emphasis.*

Frank *himself* admits that he is lazy.
Her husband is a famous composer and she *herself* is a well-known singer.
We *ourselves* are responsible for our decisions.

Notice that the singular forms of reflexive pronouns end in *-self,* and the plural forms end in *-selves.* In standard English, there are no such forms as *hisself, ourselfs, theirselfs,* or *themselfs.* These forms are considered nonstandard in both speech and writing and should be avoided unless you are using a dialect, such as you might do in writing a story.

In formal English, the reflexive pronoun *myself* is not used in place of a subject or an object pronoun.

INCORRECT	John and *myself* are going out.
CORRECT	John and *I* are going out.
INCORRECT	The director asked Carol and *myself* to read the script.
CORRECT	The director asked Carol and *me* to read the script.

Myself is sometimes used as a subject or an object pronoun in informal usage, but even in these cases the use of the correct subject or object pronoun is preferred. Referring to yourself as *myself* rather than as *I* or *me* does *not* make you sound more polite or more modest.

Circle the pronoun that most logically and correctly completes each sentence. Apply the rules of formal English usage. This exercise covers only the rules in Lesson 18.

1. He is a better athlete than (I, me).

2. They walked to the store by (theirselfs, theirselves, themselves).

3. The city controller (himself, hisself) made the request.

4. Rebecca studies more than (we, us).

5. My father (himself, hisself) is going on the trip.

6. Bobby and (I, me) like to run the track every morning.

7. The children built the city all by (theirselfs, theirselves, themselves).

8. Rick loves to swim each morning all by (himself, hisself).

9. That boy can catch a ball better than (I, me).

10. We earn more than (they, them).

11. Do you study as much as (I, me)?

12. Did the play's sets delight you as much as they did (I, me)?

13. Kevin reads much more than (I, me).

14. Yoli and her brother work a lot harder than (we, us).

15. The teachers and students (theirselfs, theirselves, themselves) built the experimental car for the science fair.

16. He likes to drive more than (I, me) do.

Harcourt Brace & Company

17. Give the book to Phillip or (me, myself).

18. We planted the vegetable garden (ourselfs, ourselves).

19. That pilot has had far more adventures than (I, me).

20. They recorded that song all by (theirselfs, theirselves, themselves).

In the essay below, cross out the pronoun errors and replace them with the correct forms. This exercise covers Lessons 17 and 18.

Have you ever bought a new car? My family and myself decided it was time to get rid of our old jalopy. I liked that old car, but my family, they didn't like all the repair bills. So, off we all went to the new car dealership.

If anyone likes a deal better than me, it's my dad. Well, this salesman, he had told my dad over the phone that he had just the car we wanted. My dad told my mother and I that it was worth the hour-long drive to the dealership.

I myself thought the car was pretty nice, and my dad just loved it. Then, the really hard negotiations started. My brothers and sisters and me, we must have waited a good two hours for my parents to talk to all those salespeople. I was getting pretty bored, but even more than me, my baby sister was going crazy.

Suddenly, my dad came in looking red as a beet. "Out, we're getting out of here!" he shouted. It turned out that they had hassled over the price for almost two hours until my dad and mom, they learned the year of the car was one year older than what they had been told on the phone. That's a pretty sneaky way to take advantage of consumers.

My family and me did finally get a new car at a different dealership. The saleswoman who sold us the car was more honest than our first salesperson and more helpful than him too. Us consumers need to be very careful.

Cross out any pronoun errors in the following paragraphs, and replace them with the correct forms. This exercise covers rules from Lessons 17 and 18.

My brother and me decided to get our father a pet. My father, he has been lonely since our mother died about a year ago. Between my brother and I, us two must spend thirty hours a week visiting our father. Nobody loves my father better than me, but I wanted some time for myself. We thought that a pet could help keep him company and give my brother and I some more free time.

We decided to get our father an older dog rather than a puppy. But between you and I, adopting a dog was not what we had expected. All the facilities with dogs to adopt gave my brother and myself a very bad time. They acted as if they knew everything about dogs and as if us two brothers were stupid.

They asked my brother and I so many questions that our heads began to spin. They wanted to know my father's work sched-ule, the layout of his house, how much money he had, and much more.

Thankfully, we did get our father a dog. He was very pleased and gave my brother and I a huge hug. I guess it was truly worth all the trouble.

Agreement of Pronouns with Their Antecedents

Agreement in Number

Like nouns, pronouns may be either singular or plural, depending upon whether they refer to one or more than one person or thing. Following are the subject, object, and possessive pronouns you have learned, divided into singular and plural categories.

Singular Pronouns

Subject	*Object*	*Possessive*
I	me	my, mine
you	you	your, yours,
he	him	his
she	her	her, hers
it	it	its

Plural Pronouns

Subject	Object	Possessive
we	us	our, ours
you	you	your, yours
they	them	their, theirs

Just as a subject must agree in number with its verb, a pronoun must agree in number with its antecedent. (The **antecedent,** you will remember, is the noun to which the pronoun refers.) In other words, if the antecedent is *singular,* the pronoun must be *singular.* If the antecedent is *plural,* the pronoun must be *plural.*

Study the following sentences, in which both the pronouns and their antecedents have been italicized.

> Because the *teacher* is ill, *she* will not be at school today.
> Because the *teachers* are ill, *they* will not be at school today.

Obviously, few people would make pronoun agreement errors in the above sentences since *teacher* is clearly singular, and *teachers* is clearly plural. However, people often make pronoun agreement errors in cases like the following:

INCORRECT   If an airline *passenger* wants to be certain not to miss *their* flight, *they* should arrive at the airport an hour before the scheduled departure time.

CORRECT   If an airline *passenger* wants to be certain not to miss the flight, *he* should arrive at the airport an hour before the scheduled departure time.

Since *passengers* include females as well as males, it would be equally correct to say:

> If an airline passenger wants to be certain not to miss the flight, *she* should arrive at the airport an hour before the scheduled departure time.

> If an airline passenger wants to be certain not to miss the flight, *she* or *he* should arrive at the airport an hour before the scheduled departure time.

For a more detailed discussion of the *his* or *her* construction, see section on "Avoiding Sexist Language" on pages 220–221.

Notice the differences in these sentences:

INCORRECT   Each *student* brought *their* notebook.
CORRECT   Each *student* brought *his* notebook.

What causes people to make mistakes like these? The mistakes may occur because when a writer describes a *passenger,* she is thinking of *passengers* (plural) in general. Similarly, a writer may think of a *student* as *students* in general. Nevertheless, since *passenger* and *student* are singular nouns, they must be used with singular pronouns.

Notice that if several pronouns refer to the same antecedent, *all* of the pronouns must agree in number with that antecedent.

Before Mike begins to run, *he* always stretches *his* muscles.
If the *students* don't review *their* lessons, *they* won't do well on their final exams.

Another common pronoun agreement error involves **indefinite pronouns.** As you learned in Lesson 6 on subject-verb agreement, indefinite pronouns are *singular* and require *singular* verbs. (For example, "Everyone *is* happy," *not* "Everyone *are* happy.") Similarly, when indefinite pronouns are used as antecedents, they require *singular* subject, object, and possessive pronouns.

The following words are singular indefinite pronouns:

anybody, anyone, anything
each, each one
either, neither
everybody, everyone, everything
nobody, no one, nothing
somebody, someone, something

Notice the use of singular pronouns with these words.

Everyone did as *he* pleased.
Somebody has forgotten *her* purse.
Either of the choices has *its* disadvantages.

In informal spoken English, plural pronouns are often used with indefinite pronoun antecedents. However, this construction is generally not considered appropriate in formal speech or writing.

Somebody should let you borrow *their* book.

Somebody should let you borrow *his* book.

In some sentences, an indefinite pronoun is so clearly plural in meaning that a singular pronoun sounds awkward with it. For example,

Everyone on this block must be wealthy because *they* all drive a Lexus or a Mercedes-Benz.

A better wording for this sentence would be:

The people on this block must be wealthy because they all drive a Lexus or a Mercedes-Benz.

Avoiding Sexist Language

Although the matching of singular pronouns with singular antecedents is a grammatical problem, a usage problem may occur if the antecedent of a singular pronoun refers to both sexes. In the past, singular masculine pronouns were used to refer to antecedents such as *worker* or *student* even if these antecedents included women as well as men. Now, many writers prefer to use forms that include both sexes, such as *he or she* or *his or her* in order to avoid excluding females.

Each student must bring his or her books to class each day.
Everyone needs to consider his or her options.

A simpler format is to make both the pronoun and its antecedent plural.

All *students* must bring *their* books to class each day.

Avoiding sexist language is a problem of usage, not of grammar. In order to simplify the rules for you while you are still studying grammar, most of the exercises in this unit will offer you the choice between one singular pronoun (either masculine or feminine) and one plural pronoun. For example,

Each orchestra member needs (her, their) instrument.

Everyone should mark (his, their) ballot.

Harcourt Brace & Company

Which pronouns would be correct in the following sentences according to the rules of formal English usage?

Neither of the professors had (her, their) office hours at a time convenient for me.

Someone has forgotten to turn off (his, their) car's lights.

Each of the actors knew (her, their) part well.

An astronaut must spend hours training for (his, their) career.

Each of the children said that (she, they) had loved the theatrical performance.

Only a member may bring (her, their) friends to the event.

Agreement in Person

In grammar, pronouns are classified into groups called **persons. First person** refers to the person who is speaking. **Second person** is the person being spoken to. **Third person** is the person or thing being spoken about. Below is a chart of subject pronouns grouped according to person.

	Singular	*Plural*
first person	I	we
second person	you	you
third person	he, she, it	they

All nouns are considered third person (either singular or plural) because nouns can be replaced by third-person pronouns (for example, *Susie* = *she; a car* = *it; babysitters* = *they*).

Just as a pronoun and its antecedent must agree in number, they must also agree in person. Agreement in person becomes a problem only when the second-person pronoun *you* is incorrectly used with a third-person antecedent. Study the following examples:

INCORRECT	If *anyone* wants to vote, *you* must register first.
CORRECT	If *anyone* wants to vote, *he or she* must register first.
INCORRECT	When *drivers* get caught in a traffic jam, *you* become impatient.
CORRECT	When *drivers* get caught in a traffic jam, *they* become impatient.

This type of mistake is called a **shift in person** and is considered a serious grammatical error.

In addition to avoiding shifts in person within individual sentences, you should try to be consistent in your use of person when you are writing essays. In general, an entire essay is written in the same person. If, for example, you are writing an essay about the special problems faced by students who work full-time, you will probably use either the first or the third person. You should avoid shifts into the second person (*you*) since *you* refers to the reader of your paper and not to the students you are writing about.

INCORRECT	*Students* who work full-time have special concerns. For example, *you* must arrange *your* classes to fit *your* work schedule.
CORRECT	*Students* who work full-time have special concerns. For example, *they* must arrange *their* classes to fit *their* work schedule.

Circle the pronoun that correctly completes each sentence.

The zoo has extended its hours so that patrons may visit when (your, his, their) schedules allow.

Participants must bring tickets to the front office or else (you, he, they) will forfeit (your, his, their) chance to win the free gift.

Pay close attention; (your, his, their) final exam grade depends on following the directions carefully.

Harcourt Brace & Company

Circle the pronoun that correctly completes each sentence. Apply the rules of the formal English usage. Sentences 1–10 cover the rules from Lesson 19 only.

1. Each member of the club brought (his, their) agenda.

2. If a citizen forgets to vote, (you, he, they) forfeits an important privilege.

3. Neither of them had brought (his, their) books.

4. Everybody chose to contribute (his, their) two cents worth into the discussion.

5. Everyone must pay for (her, their) ticket in advance.

6. No one yet knows (his, their) grade on the final exam.

7. Has someone left (her, their) briefcase on the chair?

8. Either Bill or Sam should bring (his, their) notes to class.

9. No citizen should avoid reading (his, their) voter's pamphlet.

10. The philosopher and the poet expressed (his, their, its) ideas differently.

Sentences 11–20 cover the rules in Lessons 17–19.

11. He dances better than (we, us).

12. Theresa and (I, me, myself) walk to school each day.

13. Between you and (I, me), this election is a sham.

14. Each of those professors considers rewards for (your, his, their) best students.

15. Provide instructions to the faculty and (we, us).

16. These cookies are for you and (he, him).

17. Place all those packages between Randy and (I, me).

18. The difference between Sarah and (I, me, myself) is that she has played soccer since she was a child.

19. Roberto and (myself, me, I) always remember our mom's birthday.

20. The rock concert was so exciting that we completely forgot about (he, him).

Harcourt Brace & Company

If a sentence contains an error in pronoun usage, cross out the incorrect pronoun, and write in the correct form. Some sentences contain more than one error. If a sentence contains no pronoun errors, label it *C* for *correct*. Apply the rules of formal English usage. This exercise covers Lessons 17–19.

1. Everybody needs to bring their books to class.

2. Between you and I, that movie was simply awful!

3. I just know we can play baseball better than them.

4. Although we all seem to complain about the state of things, you need to act in order to make change happen.

5. I care deeply about you and him.

6. Each one must recognize the value of their participation.

7. My brother and myself often take that seaside bike path.

8. Did you hand the tickets to Bob and them?

9. Someone left their shoes where somebody could get hurt.

10. Students must bring your registration receipts to the first class meeting.

11. The manager brought coffee and croissants for Meg and he.

12. Neither you nor me should be watching so much TV.

13. He likes chocolate cake with whipped cream and lots of ice cream more than me.

14. People on diets often spend their time dreaming of fattening foods.

15. My doctor says that we should eat healthfully and that you should concentrate more on exercise and less on dieting.

16. My friends and me, however, have trouble thinking about exercise and healthful food when all you want to do is eat french fries and other junk food.

17. A serious musician needs to practice almost all of their free time.

18. If a person has discipline, you will succeed.

19. Everybody knows their limits.

20. No one who is thoughtful should forget to give to a worthwhile charity.

Part One. Complete the following sentences by adding a pronoun. Be sure your choice of pronoun agrees in number with its antecedent. Apply the rules of formal English usage. The first sentence has been done as an example.

1. She sings better than _I_.

2. The teacher gave the papers to Cassandra and _____.

3. In a race between Rob and _____, he's the better athlete.

4. The children played the game much better than _____.

5. The religious service made all of _____ feel peaceful.

6. Each student should support _____ school's team.

7. He sat near Rachel, Betty, and _____.

8. Everybody wants _____ goals to come true.

9. Not one of us could remember _____ phone number.

10. That other team could bat much better than _____.

Part Two. For each sentence below, write a second sentence containing at least two pronouns that refer to nouns or pronouns in the first sentence. Circle these pronouns. Use formal usage. The first pair of sentences has been done as an example.

11. Julia took her son to get vaccinated.

(She) wanted (him) to be protected from disease.

12. Rebecca gave flowers to Francesca and Denise.

_____

Harcourt Brace & Company

13. Did you see the ice skater perform that incredible leap?

_____

_____

14. Allen is learning Spanish with Debbie.

_____

_____

15. Benjy bought a new video game for his friends.

_____

_____

16. Diane learned to dance with Colin.

_____

_____

Order of Pronouns and Spelling of Possessives

Order of Pronouns

When you are referring to someone else and to yourself in the same sentence, mention the other person's name (or the pronoun that replaces the name) before you mention your own.

INCORRECT	*I* and *George* are brothers.
CORRECT	*George* and *I* are brothers.
INCORRECT	You can borrow five dollars from *me* or *her.*
CORRECT	You can borrow five dollars from *her* or *me.*

The construction is actually not a rule of grammar; rather, it is considered a matter of courtesy.

Possessive Pronouns

Here is a list of possessive pronouns that you have already studied. This time, look carefully at how they are spelled and punctuated.

Harcourt Brace & Company

	Singular	*Plural*
first person	my, mine	our, ours
second person	your, yours	your, yours
third person	his	their, theirs
	her, hers	
	its	

Possessive pronouns do not contain apostrophes.

INCORRECT	The beach blanket was *her's*.
CORRECT	The beach blanket was *hers*.

Be especially careful not to confuse the possessive pronoun *its* with the contraction *it's* (it is).

INCORRECT	The car wouldn't start because *it's* battery was dead.
CORRECT	The car wouldn't start because *its* battery was dead.

Another source of confusion is the apostrophe which indicates the omitted letters in contractions. For example, the apostrophe in *don't* represents the missing *o* from *do not*. Some contractions of pronouns and verbs have the same pronunciations as certain possessive pronouns. These pairs of words sound alike but differ in meaning. Don't confuse them in your writing.

who's–whose

> *Who's* he? = *Who is* he?
> *Whose* magazine is this? (possessive)

you're–your

> *You're* looking well. = *You are* looking well.
> *Your* car has a flat tire. (possessive)

they're–their

> *They're* coming to the party. = *They are* coming to the party.
> *Their* exhibit won the prize. (possessive)

Circle the pronoun that correctly completes each sentence.

That dog is (hers, her's).

(Whose, Who's) car is blocking the driveway?

The team just received (its, it's) award.

(Your, You're) a happy person.

The new house is (theirs, their's).

A final note: When you do pronoun exercises, or when you use pronouns in your own writing, remember to apply the rules you have learned. If you rely on what "sounds right," your instincts may only supply those pronouns that would be appropriate in *informal* English.

Harcourt Brace & Company

If a sentence contains an error in pronoun usage, cross out the incorrect pronoun, and write in the correct form. Some sentences may contain more than one error. If a sentence contains no pronoun errors, label it *C* for *correct*. Apply the rules of formal English usage. Sentences 1–10 cover the rules in Lesson 20 only.

1. That dog is her's, I think.

2. Who's report did you like the best?

3. No one knows what it's name is.

4. Its too late to turn in your composition.

5. Their several different answers to that question.

6. They're singing in the next performance.

7. Me and my brother love to watch TV together.

8. Who's next in line, please?

9. Their report was probably the most impressive one there.

10. The audience loudly applauded me and the other performers.

Sentences 11–20 cover rules from Lessons 17–20.

11. Building that subway has made many of we workers nervous.

12. In this company, each of the department heads turns in their report at the beginning of the month.

13. Don't forget to give Peter and I your evaluation.

14. José decided to speak to Yoli and I about the problem.

15. Make sure each child has turned in their emergency card.

16. Don't be afraid to report they're comments to us.

17. Incredible things always seem to happen over their.

18. No one yet knows who's puppy that is.

19. Its very exciting to watch children begin to learn.

20. Nobody wants their report read to the class.

Part One. If a sentence contains an error in pronoun usage, cross out the incorrect pronoun and write in the correct form. Some sentences may contain more than one error. If a sentence contains no pronoun errors, label it *C* for *correct*. Apply the rules of formal English usage. This exercise covers Lessons 17–20.

1. The problem with you and he is you two talk too much!

2. Whose the boy dancing with Maria?

3. If a citizen fails to vote, they give up their most important civic duty.

4. If he's a better player than her, its only because he works very hard.

5. Is that car your's?

6. Their arriving on the next plane.

7. Tomorrow, who's going to offer to clean their room?

8. It's too late to worry about studying for the test.

9. I and Pedro want to work on computers.

10. Did you know which web page is their's?

11. If they're book is so good, their going to be famous.

12. Everyone wants they're true love to come soon.

13. The bank closes it's doors at six P.M.

Part Two. Construct your own sentences using pronouns according to the following directions.

1. Write a sentence containing a comparison with the conjunction *than* and a *subject pronoun.*

_____

2. Write a sentence that has two subjects: a noun and a *subject pronoun.*

_____

3. Write a sentence about yourself, using the pronoun *myself* correctly.

_____

4. Write a sentence containing *everyone* as a subject and a *possessive pronoun* agreeing with *everyone.*

_____

5. Write a sentence using both *your* and *you're.*

_____

6. Write a sentence using *who's.*

_____

7. Write a sentence using both *its* and *it's.*

_____

8. Write a sentence using *whose.*

_____

9. Write a sentence using the pronoun *us* followed by a plural noun.

_____

10. Write a sentence using the pronoun *we* followed by a plural noun.

_____

Cross out any pronoun errors that you find in the following paragraphs, and write in the correct forms. Apply the rules of formal English usage.

1. My boyfriend and me have very different tastes in movies. Although us two get along in so many other ways, we never agree on which movie to see. I myself love foreign movies and dramas; my boyfriend does not. He likes to see action and horror movies. What is a woman to do? Between you and I, I'd rather see films with my girl-friends, but out of love, I'll go with him to at least one scary film.

2. If people have ever been to the desert, you know how very beautiful it is. Its one of my favorite places. I used to love the ocean until I spent an afternoon in the high desert. Theres a special beauty in the designs made by the cactus. I find a simplicity and peace in the desert that eludes me in other locales. When my friends and me went to the desert, we were lucky enough to go in the spring. Nature blessed my friends and I with a gorgeous panorama of wildflowers. I don't believe its anything Ill ever forget.

Correct any errors you may find in the following paragraphs. These paragraphs reflect the rules covered in Unit Five.

1. Americans, they care a great deal about they're animals. There are, probably, as many different kinds of pets as there are people. Who's to say which pet is better than another? Anybody whose loved a pet knows how much they care for they're animal. Because a great many people are not marrying and creating families, pets are becoming your family. My friend, she's not married, and she will never have children. She has six cats that she absolutely adores. Me and my family visit her often, and it's usually very much like a circus. Its almost impossible to describe the chaos that awaits the family and I. I think my friend must have much more patience than me; not only is her home filled with these little animals, but it tends to have toys everywhere. What is probably the hardest for the family and I is handling the odor of all those animals. Yet, despite these problems each person must make their way in life, and my dear friend makes her's with lots of cats.

2. Someone I know has a snake for a pet. Its a boa constrictor that my friend named Mandy. My friends, we sometimes visit Mandy when its time for her to get fed; you can see her get fed once a week. My buddy usually calls me and my friends the day before Mandy is to be fed. Us friends have to prepare ourselfs for this visit. Mandy usually eats a small live creature for supper. Sometimes its a mouse or a rat. Between my friends and I, this event could be better left unattended. We'd like our friend to reconsider his choice of pets. Possibly next time he'll consider something simple, like a rhino or walrus.

3. My sister and myself just love our dog. There's no creature in the world who makes us happier than him. Me and my sister, we have collected a small fortune of coins in an old piggy bank just to buy gifts for our dog. Its a great joy to wander into the pet store with a bag full of nickels, dimes, and quarters and find surprises for we and the dog. Once my sister, she found our pet a sweater for the cool winter months. Another time, I must have been looking harder than her because I actually discovered dog sunglasses. The choice of what to purchase, however, was actually her's because we alternate visits, just to be fair. Everyone has their own taste and fancies. I was hoping her's would agree with mine. She found the glasses as silly and wonderful as me. I think that caring for our pet is nice, but even nicer is the love between her and I.

Harcourt Brace & Company

CAPITALIZATION, MORE PUNCTUATION, PLACEMENT OF MODIFIERS, PARALLEL STRUCTURE, AND IRREGULAR VERBS

Capitalization

The general principle behind capitalization is that **proper nouns** (names of *specific* persons, places, or things) are capitalized. **Common nouns** (names of *general* persons, places, or things) are *not* capitalized.

Study the following sentences, each of which illustrates a rule of capitalization.

1. Capitalize all parts of a person's name.

That man is *John Allen Ford.*

2. Capitalize the titles of relatives only when the titles precede the person's name or when they take the place of a person's name

Our favorite relative is *Uncle* Max.
Are you ready, *Mother?*
but
My *mother* and *father* are retired.

The same rule applies to professional titles.

We saw *Doctor Johnson* the market.
but
I must see a *d*octor soon.

3. Capitalize the names of streets, cities, and states.

Deirdre moved to 418 *Palm Avenue, Placerville, California.*

4. Capitalize the names of countries, languages, and ethnic groups.

The two languages spoken most frequently in *S*witzerland are *G*erman and *F*rench, but some *S*wiss also speak *I*talian.

5. Capitalize the names of specific buildings, geographical features, schools, and other institutions.

They visited the *T*ower of *L*ondon, the *T*hames *R*iver, and *C*ambridge *U*niversity.

6. Capitalize the days of the week, the months of the year, and the names of holidays. Do *not* capitalize the names of the seasons of the year.

*M*onday, *F*ebruary 14th, is *V*alentine's *D*ay.
My favorite time of the year is the *f*all, especially *N*ovember

7. Capitalize directions of the compass only when they refer to specific regions.

Her accent revealed that she had been brought up in the *S*outh.
Philadelphia is *s*outh of New York City.

8. Capitalize the names of companies and brand names but not the names of the products themselves.

*G*eneral *F*oods *C*orporation manufactures *Y*uban *c*offee.
We love *C*ampbell's *s*oups.

9. Capitalize the first word of every sentence.

10. Capitalize the subject pronoun *I.*

242

Harcourt Brace & Company

11. Capitalize the first word of a title and all other words in the title except for articles (*a, an, the*) and except for conjunctions and prepositions that have fewer than five letters.

I loved the novel *The House of the Seven Gables* by Nathaniel Hawthorne. I enjoy reading the short essay "*Once More to the Lake.*"

12. Capitalize the names of academic subjects only if they are already proper nouns or if they are common nouns followed by a course number.

Her schedule of classes includes *c*alculus, *E*nglish, and *P*sychology 101.

13. Capitalize the names of specific historical events, such as wars, revolutions, religious and political movements, and specific eras.

The *R*oaring *T*wenties came to an end with the start of the *D*epression. Martin Luther was a key figure in the *P*rotestant *R*eformation. For most of us the last great war was not *W*orld *W*ar *T*wo, but the *V*ietnam *W*ar.

Harcourt Brace & Company

Add capital letters to the following sentences wherever they are necessary.

1. sunday's *chicago tribune* newspaper had coupons for bayer aspirin and skippy peanut butter.

2. when you visit concord, massachusetts, be sure to see orchard house, the home of louisa may alcott; walden pond, where henry david thoreau lived; and sleepy hollow cemetery, where many famous american writers are buried.

3. an important spring holiday is mother's day, the second sunday in may.

4. recently, people in the united states have been moving from the northeast to the southeast and the southwest.

5. many californians are moving north to the pacific northwest, especially to oregon.

6. i have two aunts, but my aunt mary is the one i see more often.

7. in northern spain, local languages like galician and catalan are spoken in addition to spanish.

8. sitting bull college in fort yates, north dakota, is one of approximately thirty colleges operated by american indian tribes.

9. these tribal colleges belong to a group called the american indian higher education consortium, which publishes a journal titled *tribal college.*

10. during the great depression of the 1930s, president franklin roosevelt established the civilian conservation corps to help provide jobs for the unemployed.

11. my grandfather speaks only russian, but my aunts and uncles speak both russian and english.

12. i will be staying at the copley plaza hotel, 138 st. james avenue, boston, massachusetts 02116.

13. cynthia kadohata's novel is titled *in the heart of the valley of love.*

14. is english 101 a prerequisite to journalism?

15. my favorite professor is dr. clark, who teaches economics.

Add capital letters to the following sentences wherever they are necessary.

have you ever been to a rock and roll concert? i had never gone to one, so when my friend suggested we go to a grateful dead concert, i grabbed the chance.

what an international gathering! people were everywhere, speaking all kinds of languages; I mean I heard spanish, french, russian, as well as english. But probably the most amazing sight was the market scene before the concert. People looked as if they had walked right out of a sixties movie; they wore tie-dyed clothing and bangles and rings and had very long hair.

What was also amazing to me were all the very professional people who were deadheads. We saw my doctor, dr. peters, with his french wife, juliette. then i saw my professor from my history 21 class, professor johnson. he was with his daughter, a ten-year-old girl named sue.

As I looked around the parking lot, I saw all kinds of very expensive cars too. there were bmws, infinitis, and even a couple of rolls royces. The grateful dead certainly has a very diverse fan club!

The concert was great, and we saw jerry garcia, the group's lead singer and writer. we were glad to see him because he died just a short time after the concert. What really was interesting was all the very famous people from all walks of life who really liked him. there were senators from both the republican and democratic parties, conservatives as well as liberals.

The concert taught me how universal music is. I'm glad I went.

Harcourt Brace & Company

Some capitalization rules include exceptions to the rule. For each of the rules listed below, write a sentence of your own that illustrates both the rule *and* its exception.

1. the rule about the names of academic subjects

_____

_____

2. the rule about directions of the compass

_____

_____

3. the rule about the titles of relatives

_____

_____

4. the rule about words in the titles of books, movies, television programs, etc.

_____

_____

5. the rule about the names of companies, brands, and products

_____

_____

6. the rule about professional titles

_____

_____

Harcourt Brace & Company

7. the rule about days and months versus seasons of the year

_____

_____

_____

More Punctuation

In Lesson 10 you learned to put a comma after an introductory dependent clause. At certain other times, it is customary to separate other *introductory* material from an independent clause which follows it.

With joy in her heart, the actress gave her acceptance speech. (introductory prepositional phrase)

Watching the ocean, the swimmers were excited about the race. (introductory participial phrase)

Frightened by the noise, the children ran to their parents. (introductory participial phrase)

It is also customary to separate coordinate adjectives modifying the same noun. (Adjectives are *coordinate* if you can substitute *and* for the comma.)

They own a *small,* cozy cottage.

or

They own a small and cozy cottage.

Harcourt Brace & Company

You learned in earlier lessons to use commas to set off appositives and parenthetical expressions. However, when the writer wishes to emphasize the importance or abruptness of such words, a **dash** may be used instead.

February—or maybe March—will be our last practice examination.

At the party, he sang our favorite songs—Broadway show tunes.

The **colon** is sometimes confused with the semicolon because of the similarity in names, but the two marks function differently. In addition to the colon's mechanical use to separate hours from minutes (8:45) and chapters from verses (Genesis 2:5), this mark is frequently used to introduce lists, summaries, series, and quotations which may be of almost any length or form. (Notice that what follows the colon is not necessarily an independent clause; that is, it may be a fragment.)

He is studying three of the major modern American novelists: Hemingway, Fitzgerald, and Stein.

Two things are certain in life: death and taxes.

Shakespeare said it so well: "To thine own self be true."

An **apostrophe** with an *-s* (*'s* or *s'*) in nouns and indefinite pronouns makes those words possessive. For most singular nouns or indefinite pronouns, add the apostrophe followed by *-s*.

Ben*'s* games
the dog*'s* dish
everyone*'s* responsibility
a day*'s* effort
Debbie and Allen*'s* house

        or

Debbie*'s* and Allen*'s* house

But if the singular noun ends in an *-s, -sh,* or *-z* sound, add either the apostrophe alone or an apostrophe and another *-s*.

Yeat*s'* poetry or Yeat*s's* poetry
jaz*z'* origins or jaz*z's* origins

For most plural nouns (those ending in an -*s*, -*sh*, or -*z* sound), use the apostrophe alone.

> five cents' worth
> the Phillips' house
> the ladies' room

But for a plural noun not ending in an -*s*, -*sh*, or -*z* sound, add '*s*.

> men'*s* issues
> children'*s* toys

Sometimes possession is indicated by both the apostrophe and *of* in a prepositional phrase.

> That CD *of* John'*s* is my favorite.

And a possessive may follow the word it modifies.

> Is this CD John'*s*?

Direct quotations make writing vivid. Long direct quotations, as in research papers, are indented and single spaced, but most direct quotes are simply enclosed in **quotation marks.**

> "Give me liberty, or give me death."

If the quotation is part of a longer sentence, it is set off by commas.

> Patrick Henry said, "Give me liberty, or give me death."

> "Friends," the speaker said, "it's time for a new beginning."

Three rules govern the use of quotation marks with other forms of punctuation:

1. The comma and period are always placed *inside* the quotation marks.

> "We love theater," he said, "but we can't afford it."

2. The colon and semicolon are always placed *outside* the quotation marks.

> I love the song "Blue"; it was recorded by LeAnn Rimes.

3. Question marks, exclamation marks, and dashes are placed *inside* the quotation marks if they apply only to the quoted material and *after* the quotation marks if they apply to the whole sentence.

"Is dinner almost ready?" asked Beth.
Did Shakespeare say, "The ripeness is all"?

You may have noticed in the discussion of capitalization that some titles are punctuated with quotation marks ("Once More to the Lake"), and some titles are shown in italics (*The House of the Seven Gables*). The choice between these two ways to indicate titles is generally based on the length of the work. The titles of short works, such as songs, short poems and stories, essays and articles in periodicals, and episodes of a series are put between *quotation marks*. The titles of longer works, such as full-length books and the names of newspapers, magazines, movies, and television shows, and the titles of complete volumes or complete series are put in *italics*.

Italics are a special slanted typeface used by printers. In the handwritten and typewritten papers of most students, italics must be indicated by **underlining.**

We read the chapter "No Name Woman" from Maxine Hong Kingston's *The Woman Warrior.*

I love the song "Summertime" from *Porgy and Bess*.

Did you see the episode "The Coming of Shadows" on the television series *Babylon 5?*

The *Los Angeles Times* printed an article titled "Upsetting Our Sense of Self" on the way cloning may influence how we think about our identity.

Add commas, colons, dashes, quotation marks, apostrophes, and italics to the following sentences wherever they are needed. Indicate italics by *underlining*.

1. There is only one thing you need to know about your new boyfriend he is already married.

2. I am not going to retire Michael said until the end of the season.

3. An old song from the 1950s, Unchained Melody, became a hit record again when it was featured in the movie Ghost.

4. Tommy is a healthy happy child.

5. The novel How to Make an American Quilt, by Whitney Otto, was made into a movie; however, the film made several major changes in Ottos plot.

6. A years work went into the making of that quilt.

7. During a naval battle of the American Revolutionary War the British asked John Paul Jones to surrender his ship.

8. Do you know Jones famous reply?

9. Jones said I have not yet begun to fight!

10. The PBS television series Nova presented a program titled The Day the Earth Shook.

11. Did Martin Luther King, Jr., say I have a dream?

12. He tells jokes all of them boring at every party he attends.

13. Matts car easily uses thirty dollars of gas each week.

14. The essay Somebody's Baby, by Barbara Kingsolver, appears in her book High Tide in Tucson.

15. Kingsolvers other works include the novels The Bean Trees and Animal Dreams.

16. Tomorrow Scarlett O'Hara said will be another day.

17. There are three dinner specials today roast beef, fried chicken, and broiled salmon.

18. You have a spacious airy house.

Add capital letters, commas, dashes, apostrophes, colons, quotation marks, and italics to the following sentences wherever they are necessary. Indicate italics by *underlining.*

1. after we went to several museums, we went to three amusement parks disneyland raging waters and magic mountain.

2. we were traveling down sunset blvd. when my toyota camry was rear-ended by an old battered car.

3. tourists in washington, d.c., always try to visit the white house.

4. he ran for mayor, and despite his poor financial record, he won.

5. The appliance store has a sale on maytag washers and whirlpool dryers.

6. my favorite eagles song is lying eyes, but my favorite don henley song is everybody knows.

7. when i was a child i really loved christmas; now my favorite holiday is thanksgiving.

8. the american patriot nathan hale said i regret that I have but one life to lose for my country.

9. did you know that the irish poet william butler yeats poem the second coming was put to music by joni mitchell?

10. spanish music became popular for a short time in the united states with the song and dance called the macarena.

11. the singer madonna performed the song don't cry for me, argentina from the movie evita.

12. portuguese dinners often include two starches rice and potatoes.

13. that car is it yours? has a flat tire.

Write sentences of your own following the directions listed below. Be sure to punctuate the sentences correctly.

1. Write a sentence containing a colon.

_____

2. Write a sentence containing a dash or a pair of dashes.

_____

3. Write a sentence containing the title of a book or a magazine.

_____

4. Write a sentence containing the title of a play or movie.

_____

5. Write a sentence containing the title of a short story or a magazine article.

_____

6. Write a sentence containing two coordinate adjectives.

_____

7. Write a sentence containing a direct quotation that is a statement.

_____

8. Write a sentence containing a direct quotation introduced by the words, "The director asked."

_____

_____

9. Write a sentence containing two possessive nouns: one singular and one plural.

_____

10. Write a sentence beginning with a participial phrase.

_____

Misplaced and Dangling Modifiers

Modifiers are words that are used to describe other words in a sentence. A modifier may be a single word, a phrase, or a clause. (Adjective clauses are discussed in Lesson 15.) Examples of some of the more common types of modifiers are given below. Circle the word that each italicized modifier describes.

ADJECTIVE	He drank a cup of *black* coffee.
ADJECTIVE CLAUSE	The woman *who is dressed in blue* is the bride's mother.
PREPOSITIONAL PHRASE	*With the help of a nurse,* the patient was able to take a shower.

The words you should have circled are *coffee,* which is modified by "black," *woman,* which is modified by "who is dressed in blue," and *patient,* which is modified by "with the help of a nurse."

Another type of modifier is a **participial phrase.** A participial phrase begins with a participle. A **participle** is a verb form that functions as an adjective. There are two kinds of participles. **Present participles** are formed by adding *-ing* to the main verb (for example, *walking, knowing, seeing.*) **Past participles** are the verb forms that are used with the helping verb *have* (have *walked,* have *known,* have *seen*). Circle the word that each of the following participial phrases modifies.

Looking excited, the child begged for more presents.

The woman *dressed very expensively* is a famous writer.

The words that you should have circled are *child* and *woman.*

    If you look back at all the words that you have circled so far in this lesson, you will notice that although modifiers sometimes precede and sometimes follow the words they describe, they are in all cases placed as closely as possible to the word that they describe. Failure to place a modifier in the correct position in a sentence results in an error known as a **misplaced modifier.**

MISPLACED	He told a joke to his friends *that no one liked.* (Did no one like his friends?)
CORRECT	He told a joke *that no one liked* to his friends.
MISPLACED	Sue always uses pencils for her math exams *with extremely fine points.* (Do the exams have extremely fine points?)
CORRECT	Sue always uses pencils *with extremely fine points* for her math exams.

Correct the misplaced modifiers in the following sentences.

The citizen informed the sheriff that the thief had escaped by phone.

The child clutched the old teddy bear with tears rolling down his face.

A firm called Threshold provides companions for people who are dying at $7.50 per hour.

    An error related to the misplaced modifier is the **dangling modifier.** A dangling modifier sometimes occurs when a participial phrase is placed at the beginning of a sentence. A participial phrase in this position *must describe the subject of the following clause.* If the subject of the clause cannot logically perform the action described in the participial phrase, the phrase is said to "dangle" (to hang loosely, without a logical connection).

DANGLING	*While typing a letter,* my contact lens popped out. (This sentence suggests that the contact *lens* was typing the letter.)
CORRECT	*While I was typing a letter,* my contact lens popped out.
DANGLING	*Trying to save money,* Susan's clothes were bought at a thrift shop. (This sentence suggests that Susan's *clothes* were trying to save money.)
CORRECT	Trying to save money, *Susan* bought her clothes at a thrift shop.

Notice that there are several ways to correct dangling modifiers. You may add a noun or pronoun to the sentence to provide a word that the modifier can logically describe, or you may reword the entire sentence. *However, simply reversing the order of the dangling modifier and the rest of the sentence does not correct the error.*

DANGLING	*While sleeping,* her phone rang.
STILL DANGLING	Her phone rang *while sleeping.*
CORRECT	While *she* was sleeping, her phone rang.

Revise the following sentences so that they no longer contain dangling modifiers.

After standing all day, my feet look forward to sitting down.

While vacuuming the carpet, the fuse blew.

While taking the final exam, my pen ran out of ink.

By eating well, your life will be prolonged.

Because misplaced and dangling modifiers create confusing and even absurd sentences, you should be careful to avoid them in your writing.

Harcourt Brace & Company

Some of the following sentences contain misplaced or dangling modifiers. Rewrite these sentences. If a sentence is correctly constructed, label it *C* for *correct*.

1. While taking a shower, the phone often rings.

_____

_____

2. At the age of ten, my parents divorced.

_____

_____

3. I gave a gift to my girlfriend costing a hundred dollars.

_____

_____

4. The concert finally began after being delayed for an hour.

_____

_____

5. I was served coffee with a pleasant smile by a flight attendant.

_____

_____

6. While waiting for the bus, I read a newspaper.

_____

_____

7. She served pastries to her guests that were filled with custard.

_____

_____

8. Hoping to get a good grade, my term paper was turned in a week early.

_____

_____

9. He gave her a kiss on the lips with love in his eyes.

_____

_____

10. My troubles were forgotten while listening to the music.

_____

_____

11. His job was eliminated after retiring.

_____

_____

12. While preparing dinner, I watched the evening news on television.

_____

_____

13. I bought a vegetarian burger at the natural foods restaurant that was made of soybean protein.

_____

_____

14. Our ballgame was delayed hoping the rain would stop.

_____

_____

15. I brought a present to the baby shower wrapped in pink and blue paper.

_____

_____

Some of the following sentences contain misplaced modifiers or dangling modifiers. Rewrite these sentences. If a sentence is correctly constructed, label it *C* for *correct*.

1. Joe happily walked the dog feeling peaceful.

_____

_____

2. After seeing the movie, our mood improved.

_____

_____

3. She walked down the street with graceful ease.

_____

_____

4. Looking sweet and innocent, the children sang several Christmas carols.

_____

_____

5. After washing the dishes, her day's chores were finished.

_____

_____

6. The boy walked quickly down the hill with a nimble gait.

_____

_____

7. After the ballet finished, a bouquet of roses was given to Julia.

_____

_____

8. While swimming happily in the ocean, her sunburn worsened.

_____

_____

9. She skated around the rink without a smile.

_____

_____

10. While playing loud music, our house shook.

_____

_____

11. With their arms entwined, the boys congratulated each other for their good performance.

_____

_____

Harcourt Brace & Company

Construct your own sentences using the following modifiers to describe nouns or pronouns. Be careful not to create dangling or misplaced modifiers.

1. having won the state lottery

_____

_____

2. with no hope for the future

_____

_____

3. costing twenty thousand dollars

_____

_____

4. after being destroyed by the tornado

_____

_____

5. while eating an ice cream cone

_____

_____

6. wanting to save money

_____

_____

Harcourt Brace & Company

7. while driving to work

_____

_____

8. who was tired of waiting for his girlfriend

_____

_____

9. hoping for the best but expecting the worst

_____

_____

10. written in a foreign language

_____

_____

Parallel Structure

The term **parallel structure** means that similar ideas should be expressed in similar grammatical structures. For example, Benjamin Franklin quoted the following proverb:

Early to bed and early to rise make a man healthy, wealthy, and wise.

This proverb is a good illustration of parallel structure. It begins with two similar phrases, "Early to bed" and "early to rise," and it ends with a series of three similar words (they are all adjectives): *healthy, wealthy,* and *wise.*

In contrast, the following two versions of the same proverb contain some words that are *not* parallel.

Early to bed and early *rising* make a man healthy, wealthy, and wise.

Early to bed and early to rise make a man healthy, wealthy, and *give him wisdom.*

Harcourt Brace & Company

Therefore, these last two sentences are *not* properly constructed.

Since there are many different grammatical structures in the English language, the possibilities for constructing nonparallel sentences may appear to be almost unlimited. Fortunately, you do not have to be able to identify all the grammatical structures in a sentence in order to tell whether or not that sentence has parallel structure. Sentences that lack parallel structure are usually so awkward that they are easy to recognize.

NOT PARALLEL	My chores are *washing dishes, cleaning the bathrooms, and to water the lawn.*
PARALLEL	My chores are *washing dishes, cleaning the bathrooms, and watering the lawn.*
NOT PARALLEL	I expect you *to read* all the assignments, *to complete* all the exercises, and *that you should attend every class.*
PARALLEL	I expect you *to read* all the assignments, *to complete* all the exercises, and *to attend* every class.
NOT PARALLEL	The fortune teller said my husband would be *tall, dark,* and *have good looks.*
PARALLEL	The fortune teller said my husband would be *tall, dark,* and *good looking.*

Revise each of the following sentences so that it is parallel in structure.

The steak was tough, overcooked, and had no taste.

The school emphasizes the basic skills of reading, how to write, and arithmetic.

He spent his day off playing tennis and went to the beach.

Your blind date is attractive and has intelligence.

Some errors in parallel structure occur when a writer is not careful in the use of correlative conjunctions. **Correlative conjunctions** are conjunctions that occur in pairs, such as:

both . . . and

either . . . or

neither . . . nor

not only . . . but also

Since these conjunctions occur in pairs, they are usually used to compare two ideas. For example,

My professor suggests that I *not only* study more *but also* attend class more regularly.

Correctly used, correlative conjunctions will structure a sentence in effective parallel form.

The rule for using correlative conjunctions is that the conjunctions *must be placed as closely as possible to the words that are being compared.* For example,

I must go home *either* today *or* tomorrow.

not

I *either* must go home today *or* tomorrow.

Study the following examples of correctly and incorrectly placed correlative conjunctions.

INCORRECT	He *not only* got an "A" in math *but also* in English.
CORRECT	He got an "A" *not only* in math *but also* in English.
INCORRECT	She *neither* is a good housekeeper *nor* a good cook.
CORRECT	She is *neither* a good housekeeper *nor* a good cook.

Correct the misplaced correlative conjunctions in the following sentences.

He both collects stamps and coins.

She neither eats meat nor dairy products.

He both plays the piano and the flute.

My daughter not only has had chicken pox but also mumps.

Rewrite any sentences that lack parallel structure. If a sentence is already parallel, label it *C* for *correct,*

1. The article was interesting, informative, and it had humor.

_____

_____

2. To lose weight, not only must you eat less but exercise more.

_____

_____

3. We hope either to buy a Lexus or an Infinity to replace our present car.

_____

_____

4. The weather was hot, dry, and a lot of wind was blowing.

_____

_____

5. The clerk in that department neither is helpful nor courteous.

_____

_____

6. Abraham Lincoln believed in government of the people, by the people, and for the people.

_____

7. What you have done for me both is kind and generous.

_____

_____

8. The politician's speech was long, uninformative, and it created boredom.

_____

_____

9. My English instructor told me to rewrite my introduction, proofread my spelling, and that I should eliminate comma splices.

_____

_____

10. The mother said her children must either finish their homework or go to bed.

_____

_____

11. This unit has covered parallel structure, punctuation, and how to capitalize.

_____

_____

Rewrite any sentences that lack parallel structure or that contain misplaced or dangling modifiers. If a sentence needs no revision, label it *C* for *correct*.

1. I hate washing the car, mowing the grass, and to take out the trash.

_____

_____

2. Before listening to music, the volume should be adjusted.

_____

_____

3. He wanted to see his friends and visiting his old school.

_____

_____

4. He neither liked the soup nor the salad.

_____

_____

5. She performed the piano piece with wit, skill, and grace.

_____

_____

6. You either walk the dog or I will.

_____

_____

Harcourt Brace & Company

7. The company's president wanted to hire someone who was competent, experienced, and who had enthusiasm.

_____

_____

8. After finishing our breakfast, the phone rang.

_____

_____

9. This semester both seems long and difficult.

_____

_____

10. I like studying subjects that relate to my life, that give me insight into myself, and are helping me to understand my world better.

_____

_____

11. He not only works with his mind but also with his hands.

_____

_____

Show that you understand **parallel structure** by constructing your own sentences according to the following directions. Make certain that each of your sentences has parallel structure.

1. Write a sentence using *either . . . or.*

_____

_____

2. Write a sentence using *not only . . . but also.*

_____

_____

3. Write a sentence using *neither . . . nor.*

_____

_____

4. Write a sentence naming two musicians you like.

_____

_____

5. Write a sentence describing three things you would do if you won the lottery.

_____

_____

6. Write a sentence containing *both . . . and.*

_____

_____

7. Write a sentence describing three things aliens would see when they first arrived on earth.

_____

_____

8. Write a sentence describing two things you'd like to do after you finish college.

_____

_____

9. Write a sentence describing your three favorite foods.

_____

_____

10. Write a sentence describing the two things you would do if you ruled the world.

_____

_____

Irregular Verbs

Verbs have three **principal** (meaning "most important") **parts:** the *present* (which, when preceded by *to,* becomes the *infinitive*), the *past,* and the *past participle.*

The **present** form may stand alone as a main verb without any helping verb. For example,

> I *like* movies.
> We watch television each night.

It may also be preceded by a helping verb, such as *can, could, do, does, did, may, might, must, shall, should, will,* or *would.* (A list of helping verbs appears in Lesson 4.)

> I *must talk* with you tomorrow.
> Julia should study her vocabulary words.

However, the present form is not used after any forms of the helping verbs *have* (*has, have, had*) or *be* (*am, is, are, was, were, been*). The **past participle** (see below) is used after these verbs.

Harcourt Brace & Company

The **past** form is used alone as a main verb. It is *not* preceded by a helping verb when expressing the simple past tense.

They *ran* back to the classroom.
We *spelled* all the words correctly.

The **past participle** is preceded by at least one, and sometimes more than one, helping verb. The helping verb is often a form of *have* or *be.*

She *has spoken* very kindly of you.
The batter *was hit* by a ball.

Most English verbs are **regular.** A regular verb forms both its past and past participle by adding *-ed* to the present. (If the present already ends in *-e,* only a *-d* is added.)

Present	*Past*	*Past Participle*
walk	walked	walked
live	lived	lived

Any verb that does *not* form both its past and past participle by adding *-ed* or *-d* is considered **irregular.** For example,

Present	*Past*	*Past Participle*
fall	fell	fallen
give	gave	given
hide	hid	hidden

Since irregular verbs by definition have irregular spellings, you must *memorize* the spelling of their past and past participle forms. Irregular verbs include many of the most commonly used verbs in the English language (for example, *come, go, eat, drink, sit, stand*), so it is important to study them carefully.

Here is a list of some of the most commonly used irregular verbs. In addition to learning the verbs on this list, if you are not sure whether or not a verb is irregular, look it up in the dictionary. A good dictionary will list the principal parts of an irregular verb in addition to defining its meaning.

Present	Past	Past Participle
beat	beat	beaten
begin	began	begun
bend	bent	bent
bleed	bled	bled
blow	blew	blown
break	broke	broken
bring	brought	brought
build	built	built
buy	bought	bought
catch	caught	caught
choose	chose	chosen
come	came	come
cut	cut	cut
do	did	done
draw	drew	drawn
drink	drank	drunk
drive	drove	driven
eat	ate	eaten
fall	fell	fallen
feed	fed	fed
feel	felt	felt
find	found	found
fly	flew	flown
freeze	froze	frozen
get	got	got *or* gotten
give	gave	given
go	went	gone
grow	grew	grown
have	had	had
hear	heard	heard
hide	hid	hidden
hit	hit	hit
hurt	hurt	hurt
keep	kept	kept
know	knew	known
lay	laid	laid
leave	left	left
lend	lent	lent
lie	lay	lain
lose	lost	lost

Present	Past	Past Participle
make	made	made
mean	meant	meant
meet	met	met
pay	paid	paid
put	put	put
read	read	read
ride	rode	ridden
ring	rang	rung
rise	rose	risen
run	ran	run
see	saw	seen
sell	sold	sold
send	sent	sent
set	set	set
shake	shook	shaken
shoot	shot	shot
sing	sang	sung
sink	sank	sunk
sit	sat	sat
sleep	slept	slept
speak	spoke	spoken
spend	spent	spent
spin	spun	spun
stand	stood	stood
steal	stole	stolen
stick	stuck	stuck
swear	swore	sworn
swim	swam	swum
take	took	taken
teach	taught	taught
tear	tore	torn
tell	told	told
think	thought	thought
throw	threw	thrown
wear	wore	worn
weep	wept	wept
win	won	won
write	wrote	written

Notice that compound verbs follow the same pattern as their root form. For example,

be*come*	be*came*	be*come*
for*give*	for*gave*	for*given*
under*stand*	under*stood*	under*stood*

Fill each blank with the correct form (past or past participle) of the verb in parentheses. Try to do this exercise without looking at the list of verbs in your book.

1. (write) I _____ a letter to my cousin yesterday.

2. (teach) She has _____ economics for ten years.

3. (lend) The money was _____ to me by a friend.

4. (spend) I have just _____ my savings on a new car.

5. (mean) The president _____ what he said.

6. (drink) The athlete _____ a lot of water to avoid becoming dehydrated.

7. (buy) He _____ a new computer last week.

8. (swear) The witness has _____ to tell the truth.

9. (hear) We _____ some interesting news yesterday.

10. (build) Habitat for Humanity has _____ many houses for the poor.

11. (steal) The burglar _____ more than ten thousand dollars.

12. (rise) The people in the courtroom _____ when the judge entered.

13. (wear) The children in this school have _____ uniforms for the last year.

14. (sleep) The baby finally _____ through the night.

15. (feel) The earthquake was _____ over a wide area.

16. (hurt) No one was badly _____ in the accident.

17. (choose) Have you _____ the movie you want to see?

18. (beat) Our team was _____ by the worst team in our division.

19. (lay) I _____ the papers on my boss's desk.

20. (ride) This horse has never been _____.

21. (get) Have you _____ your final grades yet?

22. (stick) The car was _____ in the mud.

23. (know) I have _____ her since we were children.

24. (grow) My teenage son _____ six inches last year.

25. (gave) The boss has _____ me a raise.

26. (lie) The critically ill patient has _____ in bed for a week.

27. (shake) The house was _____ by a hurricane.

28. (speak) I _____ Spanish to my grandparents.

29. (think) Have you _____ carefully about what you plan to do?

30. (write) Amy Tan has _____ several novels about Chinese American families.

Correct any verb form errors in the following sentences. You may wish to check the list of irregular verbs. If all the verb forms in the sentence are correct, place a *C* for *correct* in the left margin.

1. I have drived my car for many years now.

2. Did the small child lay quietly during the medical procedure?

3. Please lie those antique plates carefully on the table.

4. She had lain quietly for several minutes when she heared a terrible noise.

5. In the middle of the night, a lone hawk had flew up against the barn.

6. He had laid quietly for some time when we finded him.

7. Although he was injured, we knowed we could help him.

8. I have drove five hundred miles this week.

9. My mother has told me that I have loved animals since I was very little.

10. The ship had sank to the bottom of the ocean.

11. Did you drunk that water?

12. If that window has been broke, my father will be upset.

13. He had studied irregular verb forms, so he had choosen the right answers.

14. He has spend all his money on repairing his car.

15. I have practiced, my English skills and have became very good!

Write two sentences for each of the following verbs, one using the past form and one using the past participle.

1. send

_____

_____

2. build

_____

_____

3. hide

_____

_____

4. keep

_____

_____

5. eat

_____

_____

6. break

_____

_____

7. find

_____

_____

8. forgive

_____

_____

9. pay

_____

_____

10. shoot

_____

_____

UNIT REVIEW

**Capitalization,
More Punctuation,
Placement of
Modifiers, Parallel
Structure, and
Irregular Verbs**

Part One. Add any missing capital letters, commas, quotation marks, apostrophes, colons, dashes, and italics to the following paragraphs.

one of america's more unusual museums can be found in pasadena, california, a city that has become famous for its annual new year's day rose parade. it is the mini cake museum (all three words are part of the museum's name) located a few miles northeast of los angeles, at 432 north iola avenue, just off the foothill freeway. this is where baker and cake decorator frances kuyper displays her art. people don't realize what can be done with cake and icing says kuyper. it's an art, and I wanted to show it to them.

the museum opened on kuypers 76th birthday, june 26, 1994. it contains more than 150 elaborately decorated cakes, including cakes topped with air-brushed portraits of celebrities like oprah winfrey and arsenio hall and holiday cakes like one topped with an american eagle that is suitable for the fourth of july. Only a dozen or so of the cakes were decorated by kuyper herself; the remaining cakes are other decorators works.

besides working as a professional baker, kuyper is a traveling representative for wilton industries, a company that manufactures baking supplies, and a consultant for baskin-robbins ice cream cakes. she is also a member of two honorary groups for cake decorators the international cake decorators' hall of fame and the london guild of sugarcrafts.

the information in this exercise was taken from an article titled Cake Lady's Just Desserts, by carol bidwell, which appeared in the Daily News on april 26, 1997.

Part Two. Some of the following sentences contain misplaced or dangling modifiers; others lack parallel structure. Rewrite the incorrect sentences correctly. If a sentence contains no structural errors, label it *C* for *correct.*

1. By using a microwave, my dinner was prepared quickly.

_____

_____

2. She not only is a full-time student but also the mother of six children.

_____

_____

3. A nacho is a fried tortilla chip broiled in an oven covered with cheese and jalapeño peppers.

_____

_____

Harcourt Brace & Company

4. This report must be thoroughly researched, carefully documented, and it should have proper organization.

_____

_____

5. Hoping to increase her retirement fund, Susan invested her money in technology stocks.

_____

_____

6. The pre-school teacher read a book to the children with vivid illustrations.

_____

_____

7. The secret to success is to hope for the best but preparing for the worst.

_____

_____

Part Three: Correct any incorrect verb forms in the following paragraphs.

My friends and I were bored; we were hanging around the house trying to figure out what we could do. So I sayed to my friend Jared, "Look, let's see what Janis is doing." We runned over to her house in no time. There were Janis and her friends, just hanging out too.

"We might go to Sue's house because she has a pool," said Janis. "But we swimmed yesterday; maybe if we drived to Bob's place we'd finded him home and we could hang out there," I answered.

Janis meaned well, but she often thinked up boring ideas. Now Bob always bringed up lots of good ideas whenever we hanged out together. Last time, he thinked it was a good idea to builded a shed for our musical instruments. That taked a whole lot of skill and energy. We needed to get wood and tools; then someone drawed up an architectural plan. We spended almost two weeks building that place. When we finished, we were very proud. Then a terrible thing happen. A bad storm taked place, and suddenly a huge wind comed and blowed down our beautiful work! We keeped a picture we had taked of the shed, but, needless to say, we knowed we never would builded something like that again.

Maybe we could make something else with Bob. I suggested this idea to my friends. Someone said that if the same thing happened again, he'd feeled real sad and couldn't taken it. "Ok, then let's just listen to music," I said. Everyone looked at each other. Janis begined to laugh; then we all laughed. Somehow hanging together and just laughing made us feeled real good. I guess the best thing of all is to have friends!

Capitalization, More Punctuation, Placement of Modifiers, Parallel Structure, and Irregular Verbs

Part One. Correct any capitalization errors in the following paragraph. These errors include words that need to be capitalized *and* words that are capitalized when they should not be.

my uncle jerry is in the market for a new computer. he has asked for advice from his computer science 101 instructor, professor kim. my Uncle has been looking at compac desktop computers and hewlett packard Printers. he plans to buy his equipment at computer palace, located at 545 carson avenue in huntington beach, california, about a half-hour drive South of los angeles. according to an advertisement uncle jerry read in the *south bay reporter* newspaper, the store will be having a special father's day sale during the month of june. my uncle knows he needs a good computer because he plans to major in Accounting.

Part Two. Correct any punctuation errors in the following paragraph. These errors will involve adding (or removing) only dashes, colons, apostrophes, quotation marks, and italics.

In my comparative religion class this month, we are studying three of Asias major religions Hinduism, Buddhism, and Confucianism. Todays lecture was about Confucianism. Some of Confucianisms

Harcourt Brace & Company

teachings are similar to those of Christianity. For example, Confucius said Do not do to others what you would not want them to do to you. Confucius sayings are collected in a book titled the "Analects." The philosophers' real name was Kung Fu-tzu. "Confucius" is a European actually a Latin version of the Chinese scholars name.

Part Three. Edit the following paragraphs for misplaced and dangling modifiers and errors in parallel structure.

I have a busy weekend ahead of me. There are two major tasks I must complete: grading my students' term papers and to finish the manuscript for the Fifth Edition of *Basic Grammar and Usage.* Completing both of these jobs on time means that either I will have to stay up late at night or get up very early in the morning. I will neither have time for visiting friends nor going to a movie.

By concentrating on one job at a time, my work gets done faster. I plan to spend Saturday grading essays from my literature class that were due last week. These essays compare *Oedipus Rex,* a Greek tragedy written by Sophocles with *Things Fall Apart,* a Nigerian novel that Chinua Achebe wrote. Then, after working all day Sunday, the last of my exercises for *Basic Grammar and Usage* will be finished, and I will both be relieved and tired.

Harcourt Brace & Company

Answers to "A" Exercises

Exercise 1A

1. <u>country</u> <u>has</u>
2. <u>customs</u> <u>help</u>
3. <u>Eating</u> <u>is</u>
4. <u>Americans</u> <u>eat</u>
5. <u>meal</u> <u>features</u>
6. <u>breakfasts</u> <u>include</u>
7. <u>people</u> <u>expect</u>
8. <u>customs</u> <u>vary</u>
9. <u>soup</u> <u>is</u>
10. <u>Customs</u> <u>change</u>
11. <u>Americans</u> <u>lack</u>
12. <u>people</u> <u>nibble</u>
13. <u>snacks</u> <u>substitute</u>
14. <u>Customs</u> <u>are</u>
15. <u>Culture</u> <u>includes</u>
16. <u>exercises</u> <u>describe</u>
17. <u>looking</u> <u>helps</u>

Exercise 2A

1. <u>shows</u> <u>entertain</u>/<u>they</u> <u>are</u>
2. <u>Melrose Place</u> <u>is</u>
3. <u>characters</u> <u>work</u>/<u>they</u> <u>live</u>
4. <u>thing</u> <u>fact</u> <u>reveal</u>
5. <u>Melrose Place</u> <u>has</u>/<u>people</u> <u>live</u>
6. <u>Wilshire Blvd.</u> <u>Sunset Blvd.</u> <u>have</u>/<u>Melrose Place</u> <u>is</u>
7. <u>stores</u> <u>comprise</u>
8. <u>You</u> <u>find</u>/<u>apartments</u> <u>homes</u> <u>exist</u>
9. <u>store</u> <u>is</u>
10. <u>store</u> <u>is</u>/<u>it</u> <u>provides</u>
11. <u>Massages</u> <u>facials</u> <u>are</u>
12. <u>owners</u> <u>dye</u>
13. <u>Women</u> <u>come</u>
14. <u>Melrose Place</u> <u>is</u>/<u>people</u> <u>realize</u>
15. <u>Wilshire Blvd.</u> <u>Sunset Blvd.</u> <u>run</u>/<u>Melrose Place</u> <u>is</u>

Exercise 3A

1. <u>people</u> <u>consider</u>
2. <u>parents</u> <u>objected</u>
3. <u>Elvis Presley</u> <u>received</u>
4. <u>parents</u> <u>disliked</u> <u>hated</u>
5. <u>groups</u> <u>rebelled</u>
6. <u>Elton John</u> <u>dressed</u>
7. <u>KISS</u> <u>appeared</u>
8. <u>Nobody</u> <u>saw</u>
9. <u>Ozzy Osborne</u> <u>is</u>
10. <u>He</u> <u>performs</u>
11. <u>Ozzy Osborne</u> <u>bites</u> <u>kills</u>
12. <u>Marilyn Manson</u> <u>sings</u> <u>produces</u>
13. <u>group</u> <u>exhibits</u>
14. <u>it</u> <u>is</u>
15. <u>behavior</u> <u>is</u> / <u>it</u> <u>is</u>
16. <u>Parents</u> <u>hated</u>
17. <u>Elvis Presley</u> <u>seems</u>

Harcourt Brace & Company

Exercise 4A

*Note: As subjects, either "Americans" or "Native Americans" could be correct.

1. <u>Many</u> <u>may like</u>
2. <u>People</u> <u>have hiked</u>
3. <u>Hikers</u> <u>might hike</u>
4. <u>Settlers Native Americans</u> <u>did hike</u> / <u>they</u> <u>hiked</u>
5. <u>Old North Trail</u> <u>may be</u>
6. <u>trail</u> <u>was created</u>
7. <u>Native Americans settlers</u> <u>must have needed</u> / <u>Old North Trail</u> <u>runs</u>
8. <u>trail</u> <u>would be</u>
9. <u>trail</u> <u>might contradict</u>
10. <u>tribe</u> <u>may have traveled</u>
11. <u>trips</u> <u>were made</u>
12. <u>photographer</u> <u>was told</u>
13. <u>Warriors</u> <u>could travel</u>
14. <u>Bands families</u> <u>could go</u>
15. <u>It</u> <u>would have taken</u>
16. <u>it</u> <u>would have been</u> / <u>settlers</u> <u>had</u> <u>built</u>
17. <u>you</u> <u>can see</u>

Exercise 5A

1. continue
2. are
3. are
4. finds
5. are
6. do
7. were
8. was
9. was
10. were
11. is
12. takes
13. seems
14. touch
15. are
16. has

Harcourt Brace & Company

Exercise 6A

1. belong
2. sell
3. reflects
4. was
5. are
6. knows
7. seems
8. Is
9. practices
10. speaks
11. are
12. makes
13. are
14. comes
15. hide
16. Do
17. need
18. love
19. produces
20. were

Exercise 7A

1. goes
2. agrees
3. seems
4. is
5. is
6. appears
7. cheers
8. Is
9. gives
10. claps
11. seems
12. responds
13. grow
14. is
15. participates

16. Does
17. sit
18. rest
19. haven't
20. wishes

Exercise 8A

1. enjoy
2. wants
3. understand
4. is
5. take
6. have
7. Is
8. are
9. belongs
10. like
11. Has
12. stands
13. are
14. include
15. come
16. has
17. is
18. sees
19. are
20. are

Exercise 9A

Answers will vary; the following are sample answers for sentences 1–4.

1. I want my boss to give me a raise, for I deserve one.
2. All the tickets to the concert have been sold, so we won't be able to attend the performance.
3. The results of the election haven't been announced yet, but they will be on the eleven o'clock news tonight.
4. Susan may go to Europe this summer, or she may get a summer job.

Exercise 10A

1. <u>Because I am a college professor,</u> I
2. <u>whenever I have the time to relax</u> C
3. <u>where I spend a lot of my free time</u> C
4. <u>As soon as I get home from work,</u> I
5. <u>as though it were an English country garden</u> C
6. <u>so that some flowers are in bloom all year long.</u> C
7. <u>since I live in the mild climate of Southern California.</u> C
8. <u>as if I were in the English countryside instead of in the middle of Los Angeles.</u> C
9. <u>because I live only a block from one of Los Angeles' busiest freeways.</u> C
10. <u>As long as I can enjoy my gardens,</u> I
11. <u>where my husband often spends his free time.</u> C
12. <u>Although part of our backyard is devoted to roses,</u> most
13. <u>because one of our children is a vegetarian,</u> so
14. <u>since home-grown tomatoes taste so much better than the ones in the market.</u> C
15. <u>After you eat a home-grown tomato,</u> you . . . varieties, and
16. <u>if you do not eat Asian food.</u> C
17. <u>so that we have the ingredients for our favorite Asian dishes close at hand.</u> C
18. <u>if Japanese eggplants and Chinese string beans are significantly different from their American counterparts.</u> C
19. <u>While American eggplants are large and football-shaped,</u> Japanese
20. <u>Although Chinese string beans taste like American string beans,</u> they . . . pencils, and
21. <u>Since we also eat American food,</u> we
22. <u>plants, but . . . unless we can find more space.</u>

Exercise 11A

Corrections will vary. The following are possible answers.

1. immigrants, and
2. countries, and
3. examples, for
4. "frankfurters," for
5. "wieners." This
6. steak," but
7. beef, but
8. suey; this
9. laborers, but

Harcourt Brace & Company

10. Mexican, but
11. food, and
12. States. A
13. States, for
14. bread; it
15. pocket, and
16. chickpeas. These
17. countries, but
18. C

Exercise 12A

paragraph one:
    A powwow is a
    area since Southern
paragraph two:
    arenas, they are
    area to be used
    parade called the
    guard carrying the
paragraph three:
    dancers wearing colorful
    clothing that most
    costumes include deerskin
    feathers tied to
    dresses and carry
    dancer has a
paragraph four:
    watch as each
    numbers so that the
    dancers range in
    music is provided by
paragraph five:
    ceremonies where a
    members by distributing
paragraph six:
    start, people can
    snacks like fry
paragraph seven:
    event to see
    ancestors and passing

Exercise 13A

1. imagination, didn't
2. all, how
3. trials, however, were
4. trial; moreover, some
5. tabloids, etc., throughout
6. fact, there
7. courtroom; however, this
8. by, of course, using
9. television; in addition, some
10. written, for example, by
11. fact, several
12. was, of course, Mark
13. himself, I believe, published
14. C
15. hand, a

Exercise 14A

1. literature, the
2. Nobel, the
3. fortune, an estate of nearly nine million dollars, to
4. medicine, three
5. Prize, an
6. award, the Nobel Prize for Literature, honors
7. Morrison, an
8. novels, stories
9. Steinbeck, the
10. *Wrath,* the story of migrant farmers from Oklahoma, is
11. Faulkner, one of the greatest American writers of the twentieth century, won
12. Mississippi, the setting for many of his works, including *Fury,* his most famous novel.
13. Hemingway, the
14. C
15. winner, Pearl Buck, the
16. *Earth,* a moving story of a Chinese peasant family, is
17. Buck, the daughter of American missionaries, grew
18. Prizes, a

Exercise 15A

1. (Thu Ha,) who is in my English class,
2. (home,) which is at least 500 miles away. C
3. (home,) which is in Vietnam. C
4. (community) that Thu grew up in C
5. (community) where few children had the chance to get a good education. C
6. (family,) which was very close,
7. (family) who heard of her plight. C
8. (lifestyle,) which is fast-paced,
9. (farm,) which was quiet and peaceful.
10. (parents,) who were very understanding people,
11. (Thu,) who can be shy,
12. (girl) who was from Mexico C
13. (Angelina,) who was also new to the United States,
14. (town) that was just outside of Chihuahua. C
15. (life,) which is much more hectic.
16. (lessons,) which were very hard for both of them.
17. (friends) who went everywhere together. C
18. (lifestyle,) which became less bewildering.
19. (community college) which is in their town. C

Exercise 16A

Circled commas are optional.

1. *Little Women, Little Men* ⊙ and *Jo's Boys.*
2. 399 Lexington Road, Concord, Massachusetts, has
3. Plymouth, Massachusetts, be sure to see the historical sites of Plymouth Rock, Plimoth Plantation, and the *Mayflower II.*
4. April 18, 1775, near Lexington, Massachusetts.
5. 855 North Vermont Avenue, Los Angeles, California 90029
6. October 1, 1998, till March 31, 1999, to
7. Las Vegas, Nevada, to Santa Fe, New Mexico, in
8. October 19, 1781, at Yorktown, Virginia.
9. soup, rice ⊙ and vegetables
10. October 29, 1929, was
11. C
12. take a written exam, have an eye test ⊙ and pass a driving test.

Harcourt Brace & Company

309

Exercise 17A

1. She looked lovingly at him.
2. She gave them the gift.
3. They saw us today.
4. He wished me good health.
5. We asked her a question.
6. He told you the truth.
7. She baked us a birthday cake.
8. They sang me a song.
9. I
10. her
11. me
12. We
13. us
14. me
15. she
16. I
17. her
18. me
19. us
20. me

Exercise 18A

1. I
2. themselves
3. himself
4. we
5. himself
6. Bobby
7. themselves
8. himself
9. I
10. they
11. I
12. me
13. I
14. we
15. themselves

Harcourt Brace & Company

16. I
17. me
18. ourselves
19. I
20. themselves

Exercise 19A

1. his
2. he
3. his
4. his
5. her
6. his
7. her
8. his
9. his
10. their

11. we
12. I
13. me
14. his
15. us
16. him
17. me
18. me
19. I
20. him

Exercise 20A

1. hers
2. Whose
3. its
4. It's
5. They're
6. C
7. My brother and I
8. C
9. C
10. the other performers and me
11. us
12. his (or her)
13. me
14. me
15. his (or her)
16. their
17. there
18. whose
19. It's
20. his (or her)

Exercise 21A

1. Sunday's *Chicago Tribune* Bayer Skippy
2. When Concord Massachusetts Orchard House Louisa May Alcott
   Walden Pond Henry David Thoreau Sleepy Hollow Cemetery American
3. An Mother's Day Sunday May
4. Recently United States Northeast Southeast Southwest
5. Many Californians Pacific Northwest Oregon
6. I Aunt Mary I
7. In Spain Galician Catalan Spanish
8. Sitting Bull College Fort Yates North Dakota American Indian
9. These American Indian Higher Education Consortium *Tribal College*
10. During Great Depression President Franklin Roosevelt Civilian Conser-
    vation Corps
11. My Russian Russian English
12. I Copley Plaza Hotel St. James Avenue Boston Massachusetts
13. Cynthia Kadohata's *In the Heart of the Valley of Love*
14. Is English
15. My Dr. Clark

Exercise 22A

1. boyfriend—he or boyfriend: he
2. "I . . . retire," Michael said, until . . . season."
3. "Unchained Melody," *Ghost.*
4. healthy, happy child.
5. *How to Make an American Quilt* Otto's
6. year's
7. War, the
8. Jones'
9. said, "I have not yet begun to fight!"
10. *Nova* "The Day the Earth Shook."
11. say, "I have a dream"?
12. jokes—all of them boring—at
13. Matt's
14. "Somebody's Baby," *High Tide in Tucson*
15. Kingsolver's *The Bean Trees Animal Dreams*
16. "Tomorrow," Scarlett O'Hara said, "will be another day."
17. today: roast
18. spacious, airy

Harcourt Brace & Company

Exercise 23A

Answers will vary; the following are sample revisions.

1. While I am taking a shower, the phone often rings.
2. When I was ten, my parents divorced.
3. I gave my girlfriend a gift costing a hundred dollars.
4. C
5. I was served coffee by a flight attendant with a pleasant smile.
6. C
7. She served her guests pastries that were filled with custard.
8. Hoping to get a good grade, I turned my term paper in a week early.
9. With love in his eyes, he gave her a kiss on the lips.
10. I forgot my troubles while listening to music.
11. After he retired, his job was eliminated.
12. C
13. I bought a vegetarian burger that was made of soybean protein at the natural foods restaurant.
14. Hoping the rain would stop, we delayed our ballgame.
15. I brought a present wrapped in pink and blue paper to the baby shower.

Exercise 24A

Answers will vary; the following are sample revisions. Circled commas are optional.

1. The article was interesting, informative, and humorous.
2. To lose weight, you must not only eat less but exercise more.
3. We hope to buy either a Lexus or an Infinity to replace our present car.
4. The weather was hot, dry ⊙and windy.
5. The clerk in that department is neither helpful nor courteous.
6. C
7. What you have done for me is both kind and generous.
8. The fortune teller promised I would meet a man who was tall, dark, and good-looking.
9. My English instructor told me to rewrite my introduction, proofread my spelling ⊙and eliminate comma splices.
10. C
11. This unit has covered parallel structure, punctuation, and capitalization.

Exercise 25A

1. wrote
2. taught
3. lent
4. spent
5. meant
6. drank
7. bought
8. sworn
9. heard
10. built
11. stole
12. rose
13. worn
14. slept
15. felt
16. hurt
17. chosen
18. beaten
19. laid
20. ridden
21. gotten
22. stuck
23. known
24. grew
25. given
26. lain
27. shaken
28. spoke
29. thought
30. written

Index